OUDTESTAMENTISCHE STUDIËN

DEEL XI

OUDTESTAMENTISCHE STUDIËN

NAMENS HET OUDTESTAMENTISCH
WERKGEZELSCHAP IN NEDERLAND

UITGEGEVEN DOOR

P. A. H. DE BOER

LEIDEN

DEEL XI

LEIDEN
E. J. BRILL
1956

SECOND-ISAIAH'S MESSAGE

BY

P. A. H. DE BOER

LEIDEN
E. J. BRILL
1956

Printed in the Netherlands

CONTENTS

PREFACE

The present work has grown from lectures on the second part of the Book of Isaiah. Although a translation of the chapters under discussion, Isaiah xl-lv, is given and a series of interpretative notes is added, my aim is not to present a commentary on this part of the Bible. I know that a more competent commentator has undertaken to do this difficult job. I deal with some questions of the text and the history of the tradition in order to describe the message of the preacher.

I have confined myself to some new views. I do not anticipate a general approval but I flatter myself with the hope that my fellow-students will find my principal idea or some of the minor points a stimulus for their work on this enthralling part of the Bible.

My grateful thanks are due to the circles in which I was privileged to lecture on subjects treated in this monograph, the Faculty of Divinity of my University, the Swedish Theological Institute in Jerusalem, the British Society for Old Testament Study. I am much indebted for stimulus and encouragement, criticism and friendship.

Finally, I wish to express my gratitude to my students, Mr. J. HOFTIJZER, theol. drs, and the Rev. W. L. HOLLADAY for their help in making the manuscript ready for the press.

Leiden, Oegstgeest, January 1956   P. A. H. DE BOER

INTRODUCTION

Dwaal ik Wacht u

Second-Isaiah's message has been called the Gospel of the Old Testament. That is to say, the influence of this message has not died out. The preacher died many, many years ago, the people addressed has vanished, but other preachers have taken up his words and other peoples have listened to them. The message has been transfigured, as it were relieved of its historical frame. It has become a specimen of God's deliverance both for Jewish and for Christian believers. This state of affairs involves a kind of standard interpretation.

This high estimation of Second-Isaiah's message does not release us from serious study of the text and its problems, from penetration as far as possible into the ideas and circumstances of Second-Isaiah himself and his people. Almost every student of the Bible has devoted a study to this part of the Book. The literature on the subject is immense. Second-Isaiah's high rank in religious respect goes curiously together with a great number of problems concerning the text of the Book. Not only questions of a small character but also questions of great importance with regard to the main points of Second-Isaiah's preaching. I allude to the questions: Who was the Servant? What is the theological significance of the conception of a suffering servant? Is Second-Isaiah's message universalistic?

In this monograph I join with those scholars that consider Isaiah xl-lv a unity, without a new test of their arguments or a disproof of the objections against this theory. The purpose of this study does not require a special treatment of this subject. The same holds for the inquiries into the style and

the subdivision of the text. L. KÖHLER's research into
Second-Isaiah's style[1]) is still an instructive work on this
subject. My purpose is to describe Second-Isaiah's message.

I start with a new translation of our sixteen chapters.
My translation is no more than an attempt. There exists no
better remedy against over-boldness than to try to translate
a so-called well-known Hebrew text! All the same our translations are the proof of our ability. The translation is anno-
tated in the second and third chapter of this monograph.

In this connection attention must be paid to the variant
readings of the Isaiah scrolls from the Judean desert. An
exhaustive inquiry into the significance of all the variant
readings is out of place here, but a provisional opinion about
the significance of the scrolls with regard to the reconstruction of Second-Isaiah's message could not be omitted. I have
therefore dealt with this subject in a special chapter.

The description of Second-Isaiah's message is made by
means of a discussion of the grounds upon which the missionary character of the message is founded. This discussion
ends with a new interpretation of some crucial texts.

The description is continued by a treatment of the conception of vicarious suffering. This subject brings us into the
heart of Second-Isaiah's preaching. It throws at the same
time light on the unity of his message.

I depart now and then from the traditional way. I am
conscious of the necessity that my fellow-students of this
part of the Bible will criticize the new views presented here.
The final word is not said. We can learn from each other's
attempts and errors. On the gate of a farm in my birth-place
are written the words used as motto of this introduction:
dwaal ik, wacht u, if I err, beware!

---

1) *Deuterojesaja (Jesaja 40-55) stilkritisch untersucht, BZAW* 37,
Giessen 1923.

FIRST CHAPTER

A TRANSLATION *)

Chapter xl

(1) Comfort, comfort * my people, says your God;

(2) speak convincingly * to Jerusalem and call unto her
that her time of service is ended,
that her punishment * is accepted as satisfactory,
that she has received from Yhwh's hand
double * for all her sins.

(3) Listen! one * is proclaiming:
In the wilderness make Yhwh's way clear,
make straight in the desert a highway for our God.

(4) Every valley shall be lifted up
and every mountain and hill be made low;
yea, the uneven ground shall become level
and the mountain-ridges a plain,

(5) for revealed shall be Yhwh's lustre
and everyone shall see it together *,
for Yhwh's mouth has spoken.

(6) Listen! one is saying: Proclaim!
And the other answers: What shall I proclaim?
Everyone is grass and all their firmness * is like the
flower of the field.

(7) Grass withers, the flower fades
when Yhwh's breath blows upon it,
—surely, the people is grass—

---

*) This attempt of translating the Masoretic text of Is xl-lv is not inter-
rupted by notes in explanation of my reading. Expressions marked by
an asterisk are discussed in the following chapters.

(8) grass withers, the flower fades,
   but our God's word shall stand for ever *.

(9) Get you up to a high mountain, O Zion, herald of good tidings,
   lift up your voice with strength, O Jerusalem, herald of good tidings,
   lift up, fear not, say to Judah's cities:
   Here is your God*!

(10) Behold, the lord Yhwh comes with might *,
   and his arm rules for him.
   Behold, his reward is with him
   and his recompense before him.

(11) Like a shepherd he will pasture his flock,
   he will gather the lambs in his arm,
   and in his bosom he will carry,
   he will lead those that give suck.

(12) Who has measured* Water with the hollow of his hand
   and marked off Heavens with a span,
   enclosed the dust of Earth in a measure,
   and weighed Mountains in scales
   and Hills in a balance?

(13) Who has marked off Yhwh's spirit
   and instructed him as his counsellor?

(14) With whom took he counsel and who instructed him,
   and who taught him the right way, and taught him knowledge*,
   and who made him intimate with the way of understanding?

(15) Mark the nations, they are like a drop from a bucket,
   and as dust on scales they are accounted;
   mark the isles, like fine dust he casts* [them],

(16) and Lebanon is not sufficient for fuel,
   nor are its beasts sufficient for a burnt offering*.

(17) All the nations are as nothing before him,
they are accounted by him less than nought and emptiness.

(18) With what will you represent God,
what image will you make of him?*

(19) The image*, a workman casts, and a goldsmith beats
it out with gold and is forging silver chains.

(20) The image of offering(?), a wood that will not rot he
chooses, he seeks out for himself a skilful craftsman to
set up an image that will not move.

(21) Have you no knowledge, have you not heard, has it
not been told you from of old, have you not understood
the solid construction of the earth?

(22) He who is sitting above the circle of the earth, so that
its inhabitants are like grasshoppers,
he who is stretching out heavens like the cobweb, so
that he spreads them like a tent to dwell in,

(23) he who is bringing princes to nought, so that he makes
the rulers of the earth as the emptiness*,—

(24) scarcely are they planted, scarcely sown, scarcely has
their stem taken root in the earth, when he blows upon
them,
and they wither and the tempest carries them off like
chaff.

(25) With what then will you represent me
that I should be like it? says he who is separate*.

(26) Lift up your eyes on high and see: who ordered these,
bringing out in proper order their host,
calling them all by name, not one is missing because of
the greatness of his might and strongness in power.

(27) Why do you say, O Jacob, and speak, O Israel,
"My way is hidden from Yhwh and my course* is
disregarded by my God?".

(28) Have you no experience and have you not heard:
an unlimited God is Yhwh, orderer of the ends of the
earth*, he does not faint or grow weary, his understanding is unsearchable,

(29) giving power to the faint, and to him who has no might
he increases strength.

(30) Even youths shall faint and be weary and young men
shall fall,

(31) but they who wait for* Yhwh shall renew their strength,
they shall mount up with wings like eagles,
they shall run and not be weary,
they shall walk and not faint.

Chapter xli

(1) Keep silence to me, O coastlands*, and peoples renew
strength,
let them approach, then let them speak,
let us come together for judgement.

(2) Who raised up from the east a righteous ruler, called
him behind himself?
He gives nations and kings over to him(?)*. He makes
his sword like the dust, his bow like driven chaff.

(3) He pursues them, passes on safely, on foot, a path im-
passable*.

(4) Who wrought and did, calling the generations from the
beginning?
I am Yhwh, who am the first and continual with those
following it is I [who am] he*.

(5) The coastlands see and are afraid,
the ends of the earth tremble, they draw near and come;

(6) everyone helps his neighbour and says to his countryman*: be of good courage!

(7) —The craftsman encourages the goldsmith,

he who smoothes with the hammer him who strikes
the anvil,
saying of the soldering, it is good;
and they fasten it with nails so that it cannot be
moved*. —

(8) But you, Israel my servant, Jacob whom I have chosen,
seed of my friend Abraham,

(9) whom I take hold from the ends of the earth
and call from its corners, and I said to you:
You are my servant, I have chosen you and not cast
you off,

(10) fear not, for I am with you,
look not around you in distress, for I am your God;
I strengthen you, I help you as well,
I uphold you with my victorious right hand.

(11) Mark those*, they shall be put to shame and confounded
all who are incensed against you,
they shall be as nothing and shall perish who strive
against you.

(12) You shall seek those but shall not find them who contend
with you, they shall be as nothing and nought who war
against you.

(13) For I am Yhwh your God, holder of your right hand,
who am saying to you: Fear not, I will help you.

(14) Fear not, you worm of Jacob, men of Israel, I will help
you—is Yhwh's utterance—
and your redeemer is Israel's separate one.

(15) Behold, I will make of you a threshing sledge, sharp,
new, with teeth*,
you shall thresh the mountains and crush,
you shall make the hills like chaff*.

(16) You shall winnow them and the wind shall carry them
away and the tempest shall scatter them.

And you shall rejoice about Yhwh*,
you shall glorify about Israel's separate one.

(17) When the poor and needy are seeking water in vain,
their tongue dried up with thirst,
I, Yhwh, will answer them, Israel's God will not forsake them.

(18) I will open rivers on bare heights and wells in valleys,
I will make the steppe a pool of water, and dry land springs of water;

(19) I will put in the steppe cedars, acacias and olives,
I will set in the desert juniper-trees, ash-trees and cypresses together*;

(20) so that they may see and know, and may consider and understand together, that Yhwh's hand has done this, and Israel's separate one has ordered it.

(21) Produce your case, says Yhwh,
bring forth your strong acts, says Jacob's king.

(22) Let them bring and report to us what happens,
the former things, what they are, report that we may consider,
that we may know their outcome,
or let us hear the things to come.

(23) Report the things to come hereafter, that we may know that you are Gods, yea produce good tidings or disasters, that we may look around and be terrified together.

(24) Behold you: nothing; and your works: nought;
an abomination has chosen you.

(25) I raised up from the north and he comes,
from the rising of the sun and he calls upon my name*,
and he tramples down enclosures* as mortar
and as the potter treads clay.

(26) Who reported from of old that we might know,
and beforetime that we might say: It is right.

Indeed, there was none reporting, nor letting hear, nor hearing your words.

(27) First to Zion, behold, mark them(?), and to Jerusalem I give a herald of the future.

(28) Although I see there is none, and among those there is no counsellor, whom I could ask for an oracle that they might give a reply,

(29) mark them all, they are nothing, their works are nought, their molten images are wind and vanity.

Chapter xlii

(1) Behold my servant* whom I uphold,
my chosen in whom I take pleasure;
I put my spirit upon him, judgement for the nations he brings forth.

(2) He does not cry and does not lift up or make heard his voice* in the street;

(3) a bruised reed, but one does not break it,
and a dimly burning wick, but one does not quench it*;
he brings forth judgement in continuance*.

(4) He does not fail or will be broken,
till he has established judgement in the earth,
and coastlands wait for his indication.

(5) Thus says the God (ʾEl), Yhwh, orderer of the heavens,
who stretched them out,
spreader forth of the earth and her vegetation,
spender of breath to the people on it and spirit to those who walk in it,:

(6) I, Yhwh, I call you as privileged*,
that I take you* by the hand and keep you,
and put you to a consolation of the people*, a light respected by the nations*;

(7) opening eyes that are blind,
bringing out prisoners from the dungeon,
from the prison those who sit in darkness.

(8) I am Yhwh, that is my name, and my lustre I do not
give to another,
and my praise not to graven images.

(9) The former things, mark, they have come to pass,
and new things I am reporting, before they sprout out I
let you hear [of them].

(10) Sing about Yhwh a new song*, his praise from the
ends of the earth,
those who go down to the sea and its plenitude*, the
coastlands and their inhabitants.

(11) Rejoice, desert and its cities, villages that Kedar inhabits;
let the inhabitants of Sela sing for joy,
let them cry aloud from the top of the mountains.

(12) Let them erect lustre about Yhwh and report his praise
in the coastlands.

(13) Yhwh goes forth like a hero, like a warrior he stirs up
his zeal; he raises the battle-cry, he shouts aloud too,
with his foes he deals firmly*.

(14) I have held my peace for a long time,
I have kept still and restrained myself,
like a woman in travail I groan,
I gasp and I pant together.

(15) I will lay waste mountains and hills, drying up all their
herbage;
I will make rivers into coastlands, and dry up pools.

(16) And I will lead blind people in a way that they do not
know,
in paths that they do not know I will make them go.
I will turn darkness before them into light,
and the rough places into level ground.

These are the things I will do, nor will I forsake them*.

(17) They shall be turned back and surely put to shame who trust in graven images, who are saying to molten images: You are our Gods*.

(18) O deaf, hear!, and blind, peer to see!

(19) Who is blind but my servant, and deaf as my messenger [whom] I send,

who is blind as a day-labourer and blind as Yhwh's servant?

(20) You see* many things but you do not observe them, with ears open you (?) do not hear*.

(21) Yhwh is pleased because of his privilege, he gives mighty instructions and makes glorious.

(22) But he, he is a robbed and plundered people, they are all of them trapped in holes and hidden in prisons, they became a prey, and without a rescuer, a spoil, and without one saying: Recover!*

(23) Who among you gives ear to this, attends and listens to the following?

(24) Wo gave up Jacob as spoil and Israel to robbers? Was it not Yhwh himself, against whom we sinned, in whose ways they would not walk, and whose instruction they did not obey?

(25) And he poured upon him the heat of his anger and the strength of battle; and it scorched him round about, but he did not understand, and it burned him, but he did not consider [it].

Chapter xliii

(1) But now, thus says Yhwh, your orderer, O Jacob, your form-er, O Israel:

Fear not for I redeem you,
I call you by name, you are mine*.

(2) When you pass through the waters, I am with you,
and through the rivers, they shall not overwhelm you;
when you walk through fire, you shall not be burned,
and flame shall not consume you.

(3) For I am Yhwh, your God, Israel's separate one, who
am your saviour; I give your ransom: Egypt, Kush and
Seba in exchange for you.

(4) Because you are precious in my eyes,
you are of great value and I prefer you,
I give thus men in return for you and peoples in exchange
for you.

(5) Fear not, for I am with you.
I will bring your seed from the east and I will gather
you from the west;

(6) I will say to the north: Give up!, and to the south: Do
not withhold!
Bring my sons from afar and my daughters from the
ends of the earth,

(7) everyone who is called by my name and whom I ordered
for my lustre,
whom I both formed and made*.

(8) He brings forth a blind people, and it has eyes!,
and deaf, and they have ears!

(9) All the nations gather together and the peoples assemble:
who among them reports this?
And did they let us hear former things?
Let them bring their witnesses so that they justify them,
and shall hear and say: It is true.

(10) You are my witnesses—is Yhwh's utterance—and my
servant whom I have chosen,
that you know and believe me, and understand that I

am he, before me no God is formed and after me there shall no one be.

(11) I, I am Yhwh, and besides me there is no saviour*.

(12) I, I reported and I saved, and I let hear, and among you I was no stranger*;
and you are my witnesses—is Yhwh's utterance—for I am God;

(13) also henceforth I am he, and there is none who can deliver from my hand, I work and who can turn it?

(14) Thus says Yhwh, your redeemer, Israel's separate one: For your sake I send to Babel and bring down all the fugitives*,
and the Chaldeans in the ships of their song of rejoicing(?)

(15) I am Yhwh, your separate one, orderer of Israel, your king.

(16) Thus says Yhwh, who gave a way in the sea and a path in the mighty waters,

(17) who brought forth chariot and horse, army and warrior together,
they lie down, they do not rise, they are extinguished, quenched like a wick.

(18) May you not remember the former things nor consider the things of old,

(19) mark me, I am doing a new thing, now it sprouts out, do you not perceive it?
Surely I make in the desert a way, in the wilderness rivers.

(20) The wild beasts will honor me, the jackals and the ostriches,
for I give water in the desert, rivers in the wilderness, giving drink to my chosen people,

(21) the people that I formed for myself, my praise they will tell.

(22) And not me did you call, O Jacob,
for you rejected* me, O Israel,

(23) you did not bring me sheep for burnt offerings,
or honour me with sacrifices.
—I did not burden you with offerings
or weary you with frankincense.—

(24) You did not acquire for me sweet cane with silver,
and with the fat of your sacrifices you did not satisfy me,
but you have burdened me with your sins,
you have wearied me with your iniquities.

(25) I, I am he who blots out your rebellions for my own sake
and I do not remember* your sins.

(26) Remind me, let us have controversy together, tell for
yourself that you may be vindicated.

(27) Your ancestor* sinned and your interpreters* rebelled
against me.

(28) Therefore I profaned* the temple-officials and I delivered* Jacob to destruction, and Israel to reviling.

Chapter xliv

(1) Now then, hear, O Jacob, my servant,
and O Israel, whom I have chosen,

(2) thus says Yhwh: who made you and who formed you
from the womb will help you;
fear not, my servant Jacob and Jeshurun whom I have
chosen.

(3) For I will pour water on the thirsty land
and streams on the dry ground,
I will pour upon your seed my spirit,
and my blessing upon your offspring,

(4) so that they shall spring up among the grass as willows
by the canals.

(5) One shall say: I am Yhwh's; another shall call himself*
by the name of Jacob; and another shall write on his
hand: Belonging to Yhwh; and surname himself by
the name Israel.

(6) Thus says Yhwh, Israel's king, Yhwh Sebaoth, his re-
deemer:
I am first and I am continual and besides me there is no
God,

(7) and who is like me?—proclaim and report it and arrange
that against me; what is more than my establishing a
lasting people and things to come. — Let them report
to him over what shall come to pass.—

(8) Fear not, nor be afraid; did I not tell you from of old
and did I not report? You are my witnesses, are you
not? Is there a God besides me? And there is no rock
of which I am unaware*.

(9) All they who make a graven image are unreal, and their
desired things do not help; and their witnesses, they do
not see nor know, that they be ashamed.

(10) Who fashions a God and casts a graven image but to be
helped?

(11) Mark all his devotees*, they shall be put to shame; and
the craftsmen, they are but men; let them all be gathered
together, they shall be afraid, be put to shame together.

(12) The smith [uses] an axe, and he works in the coals and
with the hammers he shapes; and he works on it with
his strong arm; if* he becomes hungry his strength
fails, [if] he does not drink water he is faint.

(13) The carpenter stretches a line, he outlines it with the
measuring-cord, he makes it with moulds, and he con-
tours it with the circle, and he makes it like the
figure of a man, like the beauty of a man, sitting in
a house*.

(14) For his wood-carving he takes a holm-tree or an oak and lets it grow strong among the trees of the forest; he plants a cedar and the rain nourishes it.

(15) And then it becomes fuel to a man: he takes a part of it and warms himself, he kindles a fire and bakes bread, furthermore he makes a God and bows down, he makes it a graven image and bends himself before it.

(16) Half of it he burns in the fire, over the half he uses to eat flesh, to roast meat and is satisfying himself, also he warms himself and says: Aha! I become warm, I feel* the fire!

(17) And the rest of it he makes into a God, his graven image, he bends himself and bows and prays to it and says: Deliver me, for thou art my God!

(18) They do not know and they do not understand, for he has shut their eyes, so that they cannot see, and their minds, so that they cannot understand.

(19) And he does not consider, there is no knowledge or understanding to say: Half of it I burned in the fire, I also baked bread on its coals, I roasted flesh and have eaten, shall I now make the residue of it an abomination? Shall I bow before a block of wood?

(20) He deals with ashes, a misled mind turns him aside, but he does not save his life and he does not say: Is it not a lie in my right hand?

(21) Remember these things*, O Jacob and Israel, for you are my servant ; I formed you, you are my servant, O Israel, you will not be forgotten by me(?).

(22) I have swept away as the clouds your rebellions and as the cloud-mass your sins.
Return to me, for I will redeem you.

(23) Sing, O heaven, for Yhwh has wrought, rejoice, O depths of the earth.

Break forth into singing, O mountains, O forest and
every tree in it.
For Yhwh has redeemed Jacob, and is glorified in*
Israel.

(24) Thus says Yhwh, your redeemer, and your form-er
from the womb:
I am Yhwh, who am making all things, stretching out
heavens alone, spreading out the earth, who was with
me*?,

(25) breaking the omens of liars and making fools of diviners,
turning wise men back, making their knowledge foolish,

(26) confirming his servant's word, performing his messenger's counsel,
saying of Jerusalem: She shall be inhabited, of Judah's
cities: They shall be built, and I will raise up their ruins;

(27) saying of the deep: Be dry, I will dry up your rivers,

(28) saying of Koresh: My shepherd, he shall fulfill* all my
purpose,
saying of Jerusalem: She shall be built, and the foundations of the temple shall be laid.

Chapter xlv

(1) Thus says Yhwh to his anointed, to Koresh, whose
right hand I have grasped to subdue nations before him,
while I ungird the loins of kings, opening doors before
him, gates will not be closed:

(2) I will go before you, and level the swellings;
I will break in pieces the doors of bronze and cut asunder
the bars of iron,

(3) I will give you the treasures in darkness and that which
is hidden, so that you may know that I am Yhwh,
Israel's God, who call you by your name.

(4) For the sake of my servant Jacob and my chosen Israel,
I call you by your name;
I surname you, though you do not know me.

(5) I am Yhwh, and there is no other, besides me there is no God,
I gird you, though you do not know me,

(6) that men may know from the rising of the sun, and from the west that there is none besides me.
I am Yhwh, and there is no other.

(7) I am forming light and ordering darkness,
making welfare and ordering disarter,
I am Yhwh, doing all these things.

(8) Drip, O heavens from above, that the skies let flow privileges, the earth may be open so that salvation and privilege are fruitful*, she may sprout out all at once. I, Yhwh, have ordered it.

(9) Woe to him who strives with his maker, an earthen vessel with the maker of pottery.
Does the clay say to its form-er: What are you making?, and your piece of work: He has no hands!

(10) Woe to him who says to a father: What are you begetting? or to a woman: With what are you in travail?

(11) Thus says Yhwh, Israel's separate one and his maker:
Ask me of things to come, about my sons and about the work of my hands you will command me?

(12) I made the earth and upon it I ordered man,
I, my hands stretched out heavens and I commanded all their host.

(13) I aroused him with privilege and I will make straight all his ways;
he shall build my city and set free my exiles,
not for price or reward, says Yhwh Sebaoth.

(14) Thus says Yhwh: The result of labour* of Egypt, and the

benefit of Kush and of the Sabeans, men of stature, shall
come over to you and be yours.
They shall follow you, in chains they shall pass by
and they shall bow down to you, they shall pray to you:
Only in you is God and there are not any more Gods.

(15) Indeed, you, Israel's saving God, are a hidden God.—

(16) They are put to shame and confounded too, all of them
together,
the makers of idols go in confusion.

(17) Israel is saved by Yhwh, a lasting salvation,
you shall not be put to shame and not be confounded
for ever.

(18) For thus says Yhwh, orderer of heavens, he, God, former
of the earth, and its maker; he established it, he ordered
it a non-chaos, he formed it to habitation:
I am Yhwh, and there is no other;

(19) I did not speak in secret, in a land of darkness,
I did not say to Jacob's seed: In vain* seek me.
I, Yhwh, speak in trustworthiness.

(20) Assemble yourselves and come, draw near together,
survivors of the nations!
They have no knowledge who carry about the wood of
their graven images and who pray to a God that cannot
save.

(21) Report and present your case, let them also take counsel
together.
Who made this be heard long ago, reported it of old?
Was it not I, Yhwh, and there is no other God besides
me,
a trustworthy God and a saviour, there is none besides
me.

(22) Turn to me and be saved, all the ends of the earth,
for I am God and there is no other.

(23) I swear by myself: From my mouth goes forth trustworthiness,

a word that does not return in vain,

to me every knee shall bow, every tongue shall swear.

(24) Only in Yhwh—to me he says(?)—trustworthiness* and
strength;

he comes to him* so that all who are incensed against
him shall be ashamed.

(25) In Yhwh all Israel's seed shall triumph and glory.

Chapter xlvi

(1) Bel bows down, Nebo is bending himself! Their idols
have become beasts and cattle*, your things lifted up,
carried*, a burden for the tired.

(2) They bend themselves, they bow down together, they are
not able to save [their] burden, and they go into captivity.

(3) Listen to me, O Jacob's house, and all the remnant of
Israel's house, carried from the belly, lifted up from the
womb*,

(4) and until your old age am I he, and to gray hairs am I
carrying you.

Since I have made, I will both bear, carry and save*.

(5) With what will you represent me that you should
make likeness,

and with what will you compare me that we may be similar?

(6) Those who clean gold out of the purse and weigh out
silver with the beam, hire a goldsmith and he makes it
into a God. They bend themselves and they bow,

(7) they lift it upon the shoulder, they carry it, they set it
in its place and it stands, it does not move from its place.
If* one cries to it, it does not answer,

from his trouble it does not save him.

(8) Remember this and be steadfast, consider your rebellions.

(9) Remember the former things of old, for I am God and
there is no other God and there is none like me,

(10) reporting the outcome from the beginning,
and from ancient times things not yet done,
saying: My counsel* shall stand and I will do all my
purpose;

(11) calling from the east a bird of prey,
from a far country the man of his* counsel.
If I have spoken then I bring it to pass also,
if I have formed [my will] I do it also.

(12) Listen to me, haughty people, you who are far from
right,

(13) I bring near my privilege, it is not far off,
and my salvation will not tarry.
I put in Zion salvation and I give to Israel my glory.

Chapter xlvii

(1) Come down and sit in dust, O virgin Babylonit,
sit on the ground without a throne, O Kasdit,
for you shall no more be called tender and dainty.

(2) Take the millstones and grind meal, put off your veil,
strip off your robe*, uncover your thigh, pass through
the rivers.

(3) Your privy parts shall be uncovered and your shame
shall be seen.
I will take vengeance and I will not come upon a
man*.

(4) —Our redeemer, Yhwh Sebaoth is his name, Israel's
separate one.—

(5) Sit in stiffening* and go into darkness, O Kasdit,
for you shall no more be called: Mistress of kingdoms*.

(6) I was angry with my people, I profaned my heritage,
I gave them in your hand, you showed them no mercy,
on the aged you made your yoke exceedingly heavy.

(7) And you said: I shall be a lasting ruler*.
You did not consider these things, you did not realize*
its sequel.

(8) Now therefore, hear this, luxuriant woman, who sit
securely, saying in your heart: I and no one besides me*!
I shall not sit as a widow or meet with the loss of children.

(9) These two things, indeed, shall come to you in a
moment, in one day;
the loss of children and widowhood in full measure
shall come upon you,
in spite of your many sorceries and the great power of
your incantations*.

(10) You felt secure in your wickedness, you said: No one
sees me.
Your wisdom and your knowledge make you back-
turning
and you said in your heart: I and no one besides
me.

(11) But evil shall come upon you, you do not know an
incantation for it and disaster shall fall upon you, you
do not know an expiation for it;
and suddenly shall come on you a tempest that you do
not know*.

(12) Stand then fast with your incantations and your many
sorceries, with which you laboured from your youth,
perhaps you may be able to help, perhaps you may evoke
terror.

(13) You are wearied with your many counsels,
let them stand forth and save you,

those who divide the heavens, who see in the stars, who
make known the new moons,
from what shall befall you.

(14) Behold, they are like chaff, a fire consumes them,
they do not deliver themselves from the power of the
flame—
no coal for warming oneself, no fire to sit before!—

(15) Thus they shall be to you, those with whom you have
laboured,
that have trafficked with you from your youth;
they shall stagger to each other,
there is no one to save you.

Chapter xlviii

(1) Listen to this*, O Jacob's house, who are called by the
name Israel, and who came forth from the waters* of
Judah,
who swear using the name of Yhwh and who remember*
not Israel's God in truth or trustworthiness,

(2) for they call themselves after the holy city and stay
themselves on Israel's god, Yhwh Sebaoth is his
name.

(3) The former things I have reported from of old,
for they went forth from my mouth and I made them
heard,
suddenly I acted and they came to pass.

(4) Because I knew that you are hard and that your neck is
an iron sinew and your forehead brass,

(5) I reported you from of old, before they came to pass.
I let you hear lest you should say:
My idol has done them, and my graven image and my
molten image commanded them.

(6) You have heard, behold, all this, and as for you, did you
report [them]?
I make you hear new things from now,
and hidden things which you do not know.

(7) It is now that they are ordered and not long ago and
before today,
and you did not hear of them lest you should say:
Behold, I knew them.

(8) You did not hear and did not know as well, nor has
your ear been opened from of old,
for I knew that you are inconstant* and that your
reputation from the womb says you are rebellious.

(9) It is for my name's sake that I am patient
and for the sake of my fame I restrain myself for you
that I may not cut you off.

(10) Behold, I have refined you but not to get silver*,
I have tried you in the furnace of distress

(11) for my own sake, it is for my own sake that I act,
for how should [my name] be profaned!
And my lustre I do not give to another*.

(12) Listen to me, O Jacob, and Israel whom I called.
I am he, I, who is the first as well as the lasting.

(13) It is my hand too that laid the foundation of earth,
and my right hand spread out the heavens,
when I called to them they stood at once.

(14) Assemble all of you and listen!
Who among them has reported these things?
Yhwh prefers him, he shall perform his purpose against
Babel and his arm [against the(?)] Chaldeans*.

(15) It is I, I who have spoken and have called him too.
I have brought him and he will prosper in his way.

(16) Draw near to me, listen to this:
I have not spoken in secret from of old,

from the time it came to be I have been there.
And now my lord Yhwh has sent me and his spirit*.

(17) Thus says Yhwh, your redeemer, Israel's separate one:
It is I, Yhwh, your God who is teaching you to profit,
leading you in the way you should go.

(18) O, if you had been observant of my commandments,
then your welfare would be like the River,
and your privilege like the waves of the sea,

(19) and your seed would be like the sand,
and your offspring like its grains,
his name would never be cut off or be exterminated
from before me.

(20) Go forth from Babel, flee from the Chaldeans!
Report with a voice of joy, let this be heard,
let it go forth till the end of the earth,
say: Yhwh has redeemed his servant Jacob!

(21) And they did not thirst when he led them through the deserts,
water from the rock he made flow for him
and he cleft the rock and the water gushed out.

(22) There is no welfare, says Yhwh, for the wicked*.

Chapter xlix

(1) Listen to me, O coastlands and be observant, O peoples from afar!
Yhwh called me from the womb,
from the bowels of my mother he realized my name.

(2) And he made my mouth like a sharp sword,
in the shadow of his hand he hid me,
he made me as a sharpened arrow,
in his quiver he hid me away.

(3) And he said to me: You are my servant, O Israel*, in you I will be glorified.

(4) But I, I said: In vain I have laboured,
to desintegration and vanity I have spent my strength;
indeed, my judgement is with Yhwh
and my wages are with my God!

(5) But now, says Yhwh, my form-er from the womb to be his servant, to bring Jacob back to him so that Israel be not swept away*, --and I shall be honoured in Yhwh's eyes and my God shall be my strength—

(6) thus he says: More indecent than to be for me a servant, to raise up Jacob's tribes and to bring back Israel's shoots*,
so that I make you a light to the nations,
that my salvation will be to the end of the earth*.

(7) Thus says Yhwh, Israel's redeemer and separate one, to one despised, to the abomination of the people, to the slave of rulers: Kings shall regard and princes arise, they shall bow, because of Yhwh, who is faithful, Israel's separate one, who has chosen you.

(8) Thus says Yhwh: In a time of favour I answer you,
and in a day of salvation I help you,
and I keep you and I put you to bundle up* the people,
to erect the land, to apportion the desolate heritages:

(9) to say to the prisoners: Come forth!
to those who are in darkness: Appear!
During the journey they shall feed,
yea, their pasture shall be on bare heights;

(10) they shall not hunger or thirst,
and neither the desert-wind nor the sun shall smite them,
for he who has pity on them will lead them
and guide them by springs of water.

(11) And I will make all my mountains a way,
      and my paths shall be raised.

(12) Mark those, they come from afar,
      and mark those, they from the north, and from the west,
      and these from the land of Sinim.

(13) Rejoice, O heavens, and exult, O earth,
      and break forth, O mountains, into singing!
      For Yhwh comforts his people and his compassion is
      on his afflicted.

(14) But Zion said: Yhwh has forsaken me, my lord has
      forgotten me.

(15) Shall a woman forget her sucking child,
      be without compassion on the son of her womb?
      Even if these may forget, I will not forget you!

(16) Behold, I have graven you on the palms,
      your walls are continually before me.

(17) Your sons make haste, your destroyers and your devas-
      tators go forth from you.

(18) Lift up your eyes round about and see,
      they all gather, they come to you.
      As I live! says Yhwh, indeed, you shall dress yourselves
      with them all as an ornament,
      and you will band yourselves with them as a bride.

(19) For your waste and your desolate places and your devas-
      tated land—indeed, now you will be too narrow for
      your inhabitants,
      and those who swallowed you up will be far away.

(20) Further, the sons of your bereavement will say in your
      ears:
      The place is too narrow for me;
      draw close together* for me that I shall dwell!

(21) Then you will say in your heart: Who has begotten me
      these?

I am bereaved and barren, exiled and put away, am I not?
But who has brought up these? As for me, I was left alone.
What about these*?

(22) Thus says Yhwh my lord:
Behold, I lift up my hand to the nations and raise to the peoples my signal,
so that they shall bring your sons in the bosom and your daughters shall be carried on the shoulders,

(23) and kings shall be your fosterers and their queens your nurses.
They shall bow down their faces to the ground to you and lick the dust of your feet,
that you may know that I am Yhwh;
those who wait for me shall not be put to shame.

(24) Can prey be taken from the hero?
Or can a captive of a conqueror* be rescued?

(25) It can, indeed, says Yhwh, even the captive of a hero shall be taken,
and prey of a mighty man be rescued,
for with those who contend with you I will contend and your sons I will save.

(26) And I will make your oppressors eat their own flesh and they shall be drunk with their own blood as with wine.
And all flesh shall know that I am Yhwh, your saviour and your redeemer, the mighty one of Jacob.

Chapter 1

(1) Thus says Yhwh: Where then is the bill of divorce of your mother whom I sent away?
and who is my creditor to whom I have sold you?
Behold, for your iniquities were you sold,
and for your rebellions was your mother sent away.

(2) Why is there no man when I come, gives no man answer
when I call?
Is my hand too short to redeem, or have I no power to
deliver?
Behold, by my rebuke I dry up the sea,
I make rivers a desert, their fish are in distress* for
lack of water and die of thirst.

(3) I clothe the heavens with blackness and make sackcloth
their covering.

(4) My lord Yhwh has given me the tongue of those who
are taught,
able to speak fluently* with him that is weary a
word.
Morning by morning he wakens, he wakens me the
ear to hear as those who are taught.

(5) My lord Yhwh opens my ear and as for me, I am not
rebellious, I do not turn backward.

(6) I give my back to smiters, and my chin to those who
pull out the beard;
I do not hide my face from shame and spitting,

(7) for my lord Yhwh helps me, therefore I am not put
to shame;
therefore I set my face like a flint and I know that I will
not be ashamed.

(8) My vindicator is near, who will contend with me?
Let us stand up together!
Who is my adversary? Let him come near to me!

(9) Mark my lord Yhwh, he helps me; who will declare me
guilty?
Mark those all, they will fall asunder like a garment, the
moth will eat them up.

(10) Who among you, fearing Yhwh, listening to the voice
of his servant,

[among you] that walks in darkness and has no light,
trusts in Yhwh's name and relies upon his God?

(11) Mark all of you, kindling a fire, girding yourselves with
brands,
go into the glow of your fire so that you shall burn by
the brands!
From my hand this shall come upon you,
in pain you shall lie down.

Chapter li

(1) Listen to me, you who pursue rights, who seek Yhwh:
Look to the rock that you hew out and to the cistern
that you dig*.

(2) Look to Abraham your father, and to Sarah who bore you,
for when he was but one I called him and I blessed him
and made him many.

(3) Indeed, Yhwh will comfort Zion; he will comfort all
her waste places and will make her wilderness like Eden,
her desert like the garden of Yhwh;
joy and gladness will be found in her, thankgiving and
the voice of string music.

(4) Listen hard to me, my people, and incline your ear to
me, my nation; for instructions go forth from me and
my judgement for a light to peoples*. In a moment

(5) my grant is near, my salvation goes forth*, and my
arms will rule peoples, coastlands wait for me and
tarry for my arm.

(6) Lift up your eyes to the heavens and look at the earth
beneath;
for heavens will vanish like smoke, and the earth will
unravel like a garment, and its inhabitants will die in
like manner,

but my salvation will be for ever and my grant will not
be broken.

(7) Listen to me, you who know right, people in whose heart
is my instruction;
fear not mankind's scorn, be not broken at their scoffing.

(8) For the moth will eat them up like a garment,
the clothes-moth will eat them up like wool;
but my right will be for ever and my salvation to all
generations.

(9) Awake, awake, put on strength, O arm of Yhwh,
awake as in days of old, the generations of long ago.
Was it not you that did cut Rahab in pieces, that did
pierce Tannin?

(10) Was it not you that did dry up the sea, the waters of
the great Ocean,
that did make the depths of the sea a way for the redeemed to pass over?

(11) And the ransomed of Yhwh shall return and come into
Zion with singing and an everlasting joy shall be upon
their heads,
joy and gladness arrive, sorrow and sighing flee away.

(12) It is I, I am he who comforts you.
What about you that you are afraid of man who dies
and of an individual, who is made [as] grass,

(13) that you forget Yhwh your maker, who stretched out
heavens and laid the foundations of earth,
that you fear continually all the day because of the
fury of the oppressor;
when he sets himself to destroy, where then is the fury
of the oppressor?

(14) He who is bowed down shall soon be released
and he shall not die, going to the netherworld,
and his bread shall not be short.

(15) For I, Yhwh your God, who is stirring up the sea so that its waves roar, Yhwh Sebaoth is his name,

(16) I put my words in your mouth and hid you in the shadow of my hand,

I, stretching out the heavens and laying the foundations of the earth,

I am saying to Zion: You are my people.

(17) Arouse yourself, arouse yourself, stand up, O Jerusalem, you who have drunk from Yhwh's hand the cup of his wrath,

who have drunk, emptied the bowl, cup, of stupefaction.

(18) There is none to guide her of all the sons she has borne, there is none to support her hand of all the sons she has brought up.

(19) These two things that have befallen you

—who is moved with regard to you?—

the devastation and the destruction, and the famine and the sword—who will comfort you*?—

(20) Your sons have fainted, they lie at the head of every street,

like an antelope in the trap, full of Yhwh's wrath, your God's rage.

(21) Therefore listen to this, afflicted one, drunk but not with wine,

(22) thus says your lord Yhwh, and your God who pleads the cause of his people:

Behold, I take from your hand the cup of stupefaction, the bowl, cup, of my wrath;

you shall drink it no more,

(23) but I will put it into the hand of those who cause you grief, those who say to you: Bow down*, that we may pass over. And you made your back like the ground and like the street [for them] to pass over.

Chapter lii

(1) Awake, awake, put on your strength, O Zion,
    put on your beautiful* garments, O Jerusalem, holy city,
    for no more shall come into you uncircumcised and un-
    clean people.

(2) Shake yourself from the dust, arise, sit, O Jerusalem,
    loose the bonds from your neck, O captive Zionit,

(3) for thus says Yhwh: Without charge you were sold,
    without money you shall be redeemed as well.

(4) For thus says my lord Yhwh: My people went down
    into Egypt to sojourn there at the first, and the Assy-
    rians oppressed them at the last*,

(5) but now, what about me* here?
    —is Yhwh's utterance—
    that my people are taken away without charge,
    their rulers are boastful
    —is Yhwh's utterance—
    and continually all the day is my name despised.

(6) Therefore my people shall know my name*;
    therefore in that day, for I am he who speaks: here
    I am!*

(7) How beautiful upon the mountains are the feet of him
    who brings good tidings, who lets be heard: Welfare!,
    who brings tidings of good,
    who lets be heard salvation, saying to Zion: Your
    God rules*!

(8) Hear, your watchmen lift up their voice,
    they shout for joy together,
    for they see eye to eye* the return of Yhwh to Zion.

(9) Break forth into singing, exult together, ruins of Jeru-
    salem,
    for Yhwh comforts his people, he redeems Jerusalem.

(10) Yhwh bares his holy arm before the eyes of all the
nations,

and all the ends of the earth see the salvation of our God.

(11) Depart, depart, go out thence, do not touch an unclean
thing, go out from the midst of her, purify yourselves,
you who bear the vessels of Yhwh.

(12) For without panic you shall go out and without fligth
you shall go,

for Yhwh goes before you and Israel's God is your
rear guard.

(13) Behold, my servant shall prosper, he shall be exalted
and lifted up, and he shall be very high*.

(14) As many are astonished at you

—his* appearance is so marred that it is beyond human
semblance, and his stature beyond that of mankind—

(15) so many nations sprinkled* him and kings purse up
their mouths.

Indeed, that which has not been told them they see,
and that which they have not heard they meet with.

Chapter liii

(1) Who measures up to* that which we hear and to whom
has been revealed Yhwh's arm?

(2) And he shot forth like a young plant by itself*,

like a root out of dry ground.

He had neither stature nor elegance that we should look
at him,

and no appearance that we should desire him.

(3) He was despised and forsaken by men,

a man of pains and acquainted with sickness*,

and despised as one from whom men hide the face,

and he did not count to us.

(4) Surely, he bore our sicknesses and carried our pains*.
Yet we esteemed him stricken, smitten by God and
humilated.

(5) But he was struck because of our rebellions,
shattered because of our iniquities.
The chastisement was upon him so that we are prosperous and through his stripes we are healed.

(6) All of us went astray like sheep, each turned to his own
way,
but Yhwh struck him with the punishment of us all.

(7) He was oppressed and humilated but he did not open
his mouth;
like a lamb that is carried to the slaughter and like a
sheep before its shearers, dumb, he did not open his
mouth.

(8) Without delay and without judgement he was taken away,
and who commiserated his fate*?
For he was cut off out of the land of the living,
because of the rebellion of my people the blow [struck]
him.

(9) And they made his grave with the wicked,
and with a rich man* his grave*,
although he did no violence and there was no deceit in
his mouth.

(10) But it was Yhwh's purpose to bruise him,
he made him sick.
When he has made atonement*, he shall see seed, he
shall prolong his days,
and Yhwh's purpose shall prosper in his hand.

(11) He shall see* because of his travail, he shall be satisfied
with his rest*,
my righteous servant shall acquire privileges* for
many whose iniquities he bore.

(12) Therefore I will divide him a portion with the great,
and he shall divide spoil with the strong,
in exchange for laying himself bare* to death, and
classing himself among the rebels, holding up* the
sin of many and making intercession for the rebels.

Chapter liv

(1) Rejoice, O barren one who did not bear,
break forth into singing and exult who have not been in
travail!
For the sons of the desolate one are more than the sons
of the married woman, says Yhwh.

(2) Enlarge the place of your tent, let them stretch out the
curtains of your habitations,
be not careful, lengthen your tent-cords and strengthen
your tent-pegs,

(3) for you will break out to the right and to the left,
and your seed shall expel nations
and they shall people desolate cities*.

(4) Fear not, for you will not be ashamed,
and be not confounded for you will not be put to shame.
But the shame of your youth you will forget
and the scorn of your widowhood you will remember
no more.

(5) For your husband is your maker, Yhwh Sebaoth is his
name,
and Israel's separate one is your redeemer, the God of
the whole earth he is called.

(6) For Yhwh has called you as a wife forsaken and grieved
in spirit,
yea a wife of youth when she is rejected, says your
God.

(7) For a brief moment* I forsook you,
but with great compassion I will gather you.

(8) In overflowing wrath I hid my face from you a brief
moment,
but with lasting devotion I will have compassion on
you,
says your redeemer Yhwh.

(9) This is like Noah's days* to me,
as I swore that Noah's waters should no more go over
the earth,
so I swear not to be angry with you and not to rage
against you.

(10) For the mountains will move and the hills will totter,
but my devotion shall not move from you
and my beneficial covenant shall not totter,
says Yhwh who has compassion on you.

(11) O humilated one, broken adrift, not comforted,
mark me who will set your stones in antimony,
and lay your foundations with sapphires,

(12) and I will make your pinnacles like agate
and your gates of sparkling stones
and all your walls of precious stones;

(13) and all your sons to be disciples of Yhwh,
and great shall be the prosperity of your sons.

(14) Privileged you shall be established,
being far from oppression, for you shall not be afraid,
and from terror, for it shall not come near you.

(15) Suppose one attacks over my head*—he who attacks
you shall fall against you.

(16) Behold, it is I who order the smith who blows the fire
of coals and produces a tool for his work,
and as for me, I order the waster to destroy.

(17) Every tool fashioned against you shall not prosper,

and every tongue that rises against you in judgement
you shall refute.
This is the heritage of the servants of Yhwh,
and their privilege from me,
says Yhwh.

Chapter lv

(1) O everyone who thirsts, come to the waters,
and he who has no money, come, buy and eat!
Come and buy wine and milk without money and without price!

(2) Why do you weigh money for that which is not bread,
and your earnings for that which does not satisfy?
Listen hard to me that you may eat what is good
and delight yourselves in fatness.

(3) Incline your ear and come to me, hear that you may live.
For I will make with you an everlasting covenant,
my reliable evidences of devotion to David,

(4) behold, I made him a witness to the peoples,
a leader and commander for the peoples*.

(5) Behold, you shall call a nation that you do not know,
and a nation that does not know you shall run to you,
because of Yhwh your God and Israel's separate one,
for he has glorified you*.

(6) Seek Yhwh now that you come upon him,
call upon him now that he is near.

(7) Let the wicked forsake his way,
and the unrighteous man his plans;
let him return to Yhwh that he may have mercy on him,
and to our God, for he abundantly pardons.

(8) For my plans* are not your plans,
and your ways are not my ways, says Yhwh.

(9) For as the heavens are higher than earth, so are my ways
   higher than your ways, and my plans than your plans.
(10) For as the rain and the snow come down from the
   heavens
   and return not thither but water the country,
   making it bring forth and sprout,
   and giving seed to the sower and bread to the eater,
(11) so is my word that goes forth from my mouth,
   it does no return to me empty but it effects that which I
   purpose and prospers in the thing for which I sent it.
(12) Indeed, you shall go out in joy and be led forth in
   prosperity;
   the mountains and the hills shall break forth into singing
   before you,
   and all the trees of the field shall clap their hands*.
(13) Instead of the thorn shall shoot forth the juniper-tree,
   instead of the stinging nettle shall shoot forth the myrtle,
   and it shall be to Yhwh for a name,
   for an everlasting token which shall not be cut off*.

SECOND CHAPTER

SOME INTERPRETATIVE NOTES

En même temps que le connu
l'inconnu s'augmente

BRULÂT

xl 1. Comfort, comfort. Cf. xlix 13; li 3, 12; lii 9; (xii 1; lxi 2; lxvi 13). No complaint but an encouragement. The verb *nḥm* means to open up new sources of life, to renew, renovate. A word of comfort causes a new beginning. The repetition —frequently in Second-Isaiah's style, xliii 11; xlviii 11, 15; li 9; lii 1; (lvii 14; lxii 10)—indicates intensity.

xl 2. dibber ʿal leb. Cf. Gen. l 21, parallel to *nḥm. leb* is not the residence of feeling but of will and power. The expression means: to speak with convincingness, promise, appealing to the motive power of the person(s) spoken to. The possibility of a new activity is presumed both with *nḥm* and *dibber ʿal leb.* Cf. too שִׂים עַל לֵב?, parallel to זכר, Is. xlvii 7.

punishment. The meaning of the Hebrew word is iniquity together with its after-effect. The idea of sin never means an act pure. "Your fathers have walked after vanity and are become vain", Jerem. ii 5.

double. See chapter VI on vicarious suffering, p. 115.

xl 3. one (is proclaiming). Here and in verse 6 the reference is to an assembly of heavenly beings, heralds, spoken to. They are to proclaim Yhwh's orders.

xl 5. together. יחדו, too in xli 1, 19f, 23; xliii 9, 17; xlv 16, 20, 21; xlvi 2; xlviii 13; lii 8f; and יחד in xlii 14; xliii 26; xliv 11; xlv 8; l 8. Used of a community in action. The adverb indicates the public character of the action. The term can be paraphrased by "in public", "in open court", "openly, frankly"; and in xlv 8, and xlviii 13 by "at once".[1]

xl 6. firmness. The meaning of the word is connection, relation and hence devotion. In our case the strength, solidity of mankind is in discussion. Beauty, or goodliness are mistranslations, in my opinion.

xl 8. our God's word . . . God's word is his act. The effects of his deeds are sure without any limitation.

xl 10. with might. A probable reading is בְּחֹזֶק . However, the vowels of the Masoretic reading remain unexplained. It seems to me improbable to suppose that the Masoretes meant the adjective חָזָק . Perhaps they preserved a second reading with their vowels, e.g. בְּצָבָא , with an army (host of angels); or, בְּחָמָס , by violence.

xl 12. who has measured . . . etc. Interrogative sentences with *mi-* (cf. too sentences with '*t-mi* and '*l-mi*, with whom . ., with which . ., vv. 14, 18, 25) are rhetorical questions, frequently used in Second-Isaiah's style, expressing: nobody, nothing, with a strong emphasis.

Measuring means commanding, having domination; the ordering activity of the high god 'El is meant here.

xl 14. knowledge. Here and elsewhere (xl 21; lii 6) experimental knowledge, experience, is meant, in agreement with the signification, "to engage in", "meddle with", "take the matter up", of the stem ידע ; cf. e.g. Gen. xxxix 6.

xl 15. he casts, from טול . Or, *he takes up,* from נטל , M.

xl 16. The local colour of the language used seems to be Palestinian. Cf. too xli 18f; xlii 11f; lv 12f. The exiles lived in their past. There may have been too some connection between the exiles and the Judean people that stayed behind in several parts of Palestine.

xl 18 and 25. The rendering *with what will you represent* I prefer to the usual translation *to whom will you liken* or, *compare*

God, because of the second part of verse 18, *what image will you make of him.*

xl 19f. The idea of an idol in verse 18b is taken up by vv. 19f. They may be considered as a digression on this idea of an image of 'El. A similar digression, also with the idea of idols, occurs in xli 7. This similarity is, in my opinion, not a sufficient ground to re-arrange the text.

xl 22f. Mythological ideas are mentioned in the same breath as historical facts. Cf. xliii 7, li 9f, 16. Both mythology and history are modern conceptions. They are not distinguished in ancient times, being both considered as Yhwh's deeds.

xl 25. separate. qadoš is here and everywhere rendered by *(the) separate one*, in order to express the incomparable and special character of Israel's God. Yhwh is both unassailable and wholly devoted to his people.

xl 27. my course. mišpaṭ is a synonym of *derek*, way. Right means judgement, the way of life of the punished people. There is, as far as I see, some connection with xl 2 in this verse. The people spoken to, consider their sins already expiated. Nevertheless their disaster, the exile, goes on. They say: Yhwh must have left us definitively, there is no end of his wrath. Second-Isaiah on the contrary explains the long period of suffering as a double satisfaction and creates a new idea, the conception of vicarious suffering.

xl 28. the ends of the earth. A frequently used expression. The limits of the earth are not literally meant but the earth as far as her ends, i.e. the whole earth. See ad xli 1.

xl 31. wait for. To wait for means at the same time depend on. See the writer's treatment of the stem *qwh* in *OTS* x, 1954, p. 225 ff.

xli 1. coastlands. This expression possesses the same meaning as the ends of the earth, i.e. the whole earth. The figure of speech presents a Palestinian, or better Mediterranean local colour, cf. Is. xx 6; xxiii 2, 6.

xli 2. a righteous ruler, or, a victor, conqueror, privileged with might to be victorious, cf. xlv 13, and xlix 24.

behind himself. God goes in front of him, smoothes the way for him, guaranteeing his victory.

He gives nations and kings over to him. God delivers his enemies to him. Nations and kings may belong together. They can be a unity indicating numerousness and might, influence, cf. Gen. xvii 6; Jerem. xxv 14; xxvii 7. In this case the three letters ירד are a scribal error. A copyist started too early with verse 3, found after having written three letters he has committed an error and continued directly with the right continuation of his line. This is the ancient manner of correcting one's errors. But a later copyist of his manuscript did not omit the three superfluous letters and still later attempts were made to give sense to them. However, a reading יְרֹד, of the stem רדד, is possible too, cf. xlv 1.

dust and *driven chaff* are symbols of innumerable multitude, cf. Zech. ix 3; Zeph. i 17; Ps. lxxviii 27; Job xxvii 16; and of lightness, the speed of the bow's arrows.

xli 3. Or, by paths his feet have not trod.

xli 4. The lasting activity of Yhwh is underlined. He does not cancel his work.

xli 6. countryman. "Brother" is a synonym of neighbour.

xli 7. This verse is a digression on the conception "to make strong", "encourage". The subject of the addition is the same as in xl 19. But the point of contact is different.

xli 11. Mark those, they shall . . . This rendering of הֵן, here and elsewhere used, tries to present the strong connection with the subject of the following verb.

There is a strong putting of the case by the climax in the verbs used here, לחם, נצה, ריב, חרה. The total weakness of the enemy is presented by four hendiadyoins, be put to shame and be confounded; be as nothing and perish, seek and not find, be as nothing and nought.

xli 15. with teeth. Two-edged? Cf. Ps. cxlix 6.

mountains and hills. They are immovable and firm obstacles. Metaphorical language for the mighty powers of the earth, the foreign nations who has vanquished the Judean people.

xli 16. rejoice about Yhwh—about Israel's separate one. גיל ב and התהלל ב. *beth objecti.* Cf. to erect lustre, about Yhwh, *lamed objecti,* and parallels, referred to ad xlii 10. The contents of the song are the deeds of Yhwh to be reported in the coastlands, i.e. everywhere, as far as the ends of the earth, as a praise of his name, of his manifestations.

xli 19. cedars and further names of trees, see E. DE VAUMAS, *Le Liban,* Paris 1954.

xli 25. he calls upon my name. Or, he is called with my name, cf. xliii 7; Gen. xxi 12.

          and he tramples down enclosures. I read ויבס גנים. I suggest that an early copyist has made an error, writing the frequently occurring verb ויבא. At once he observed his error and corrected it by putting the right letter, ס, after the wrong *'alef.* But those who used his manuscript or copied it did not understand his correction and pointed the text as we read it in the Masoretic text. The letter ס is added to the following word and this is read like the Akkadian loan-word known from Jerem. li, Ezek. xxiii and post-exilic texts.

To trample down *gannim,* enclosures, means to give up the plantations to the wind, the beasts and to robbers.

xlii 1. Second-Isaiah uses the name: my servant, parallel to my chosen, my beloved one. To be a servant of a mighty lord means to have a safe position. Jacob's unfortunate state after the disasters of the beginning of the sixth century is depicted as the fate of a servant sold to a foreigner. Herewith he is bereft of his safe position and made to a person without rights. See further chapter V, p. 90ff.

xlii 2. lift up—his voice. His voice is object of the verb to make heard and at the same time of the verb to lift up. See the writer's "An inquiry into the meaning of the term מַשָּׂא", in *OTS* v, 1948, p. 197ff., esp. p. 212.

xlii 3. See chapter V, p. 91ff.

in continuance. Or, a lasting (judgement). A judgement of a continuing strength is meant. See chapter V, p. 91.

xlii 6. privileged. See F. ROSENTHAL's excellent treatment of the term *ṣdq*, right, privilege, grant, gift, in *HUCA*, 1950-51, p. 411ff.

that I make etc. The Masoretic pointing *wᵉ*, in order to, so that.

a consolidation of the people, see chapter V, p. 94.

a light respected by the nations, see chapter V, p. 92, 95.

xlii 10. Sing about Yhwh a new song. Šir lᵉ is a synonym to *tᵉna (šana) lᵉ*, Judg. xi 40, to sing concerning, or, celebrate, the daughter of Jephtah. Cf. Is. v 1, "Let me sing concerning my beloved". A new song is mentioned too in Pss. xxxiii 3; xcviii 1; xcvi 1; cxliv 9; cxlix 1. Second-Isaiah uses the term new too in xli 15; xlviii 6 (cf. further lxii 2; lxv 17; lxvi 22; lxi 4; Jerem. xxxi 22, 31; Ezek. xi 19.). New things are not only recent but too different from the present, unexpected, wonderful. The meaning of *ḥadaš*, new, in our expression can be derived from verse 9. The "new things" are Yhwh's redemption of his people, Yhwh's new manifestations, his salvation, his marvellous deeds.

Those who go down to the sea and its plenitude. The craftsmen working in and on the sea, gathering shells for purple manufacturing, and merchants, sailors. The local colour here is again Mediterranean.

xlii 13. Yhwh's zeal is his being intensely and personally

concerned in the deeds for deliverance of his people. "Yhwh
the passionate", see S. D. GOITEIN in *VT* vi, 1956, p. 4f.
This verse seems to be a heading. J. MORGENSTERN on the
contrary holds that the vv. 10-13 are an intrusion into the
text from some other source, a fragment of a psalm composed
between 516 and 485 B.C., in *To Do and to Teach*, essays in
honour of Ch. L. PYATT, Lexington 1953.

xlii 16. These are the things I will do nor will I forsake them.
Perfecta futura. This line can be rendered too by: I used to do
them and I did not forsake them. If so rendered it is a late
addition to the text.

xlii 17. This verse seems to be an addition, probably liturgical.

xlii 20. You see. I read *K·tib*: רָאִיתָ

You do not hear. Reading תשמע instead of ישמע,
with several MSS. It seems to me possible that the Masoretic text contains a reminiscence of Is. vi 10. It is possible,
too, to retain the third person of M's reading. The translation:
"with ears open he does not hear", a saying.

The verbs *šmr* and *šmᶜ* both present the manner of life of
him who is incorporated in a covenant. Observance and obedi-
ence are conceptions following seeing and doing! The peculiar
sequence of act and obey has been observed in b. Šabbath 88a,
referring to Ps. ciii 20, where is said of the ministering angels:
Ye mighty in strength, that fulfil his word, that hearken
unto the voice of his word. And to Cant. ii 3, the apple tree
— or, according to others, the citron tree—explained as an
allegorical name of Israel: the fruit of the tree mentioned
precedes its leaves, so did the Israelites give precedence to
"we will do" over "we will hearken". Cf. too an old Jewish
saying with regard to incomprehensibilities in the liturgy:
"A pious Jew does not ask: Why".

xlii 22. Recover, or, restore.

xliii 1. Redemption can only be made by the official ransomer, the *go'el*, the former master of the slave, or, the parent who is authorised to ransom.

xliii 7. The redemption is pictured as a new exodus from slavery in a foreign country. The renovation of the people is connected with the conception of the ordering of the earth and the heavens, by using the same verbs as used in Genesis, עשה, יצר, ברא. The idea of creation, ordering, is in Second-Isaiah similar to the idea of the redemption. But the use of creation motives is subordinate to the main subject, the reconsolidation of the people. The same can be said of Second-Isaiah's references to the patriarch Abraham, xli 8; li 2. See further chapter III, p. 66 and chapter V, p. 85f. A recent discussion can be found in B. J. VAN DER MERWE, *Pentateuchtradisies in die prediking van Deuterojesaja*, Groningen 1955.

xliii 11. No one besides me. Cf. xliv 6, 8; xlv 5, 21; xlvii 8, 10. The depiction of the virgin Babylonit in xlvii who says: no one besides me, is a good illustration of the meaning of the expression. She does not mean to say that she is the only woman, but that she is unique. Each other town is of a minor class compared to Babel. Likewise Yhwh is not saying that he is the only God, but he is proclaiming his unique strength. No one besides me means: I have no competitor, no rival.

xliii 12. I was no stranger. No strange God, cf. Deut. xxxii 16; Jerem. ii 25; iii 13; Mal. ii 11. The speaker may have meant to say: when I was prophesying, deciding your future, you was not in uncertainty as to who I was. The same God who was Israel's saviour in former days is acting again to deliver his people. The meaning of the verse can be too: there was no strange God among you, i.e. it was Yhwh himself who foretelled and saved you in former days. Or, among you there is no stranger, i.e. the whole people is Jewish, believers of Yhwh, his witnesses.

xliii 14. bring down all of them as fugitives. Or, break down all the bars. G. R. DRIVER suggests the reading *bʿriḥim*, Syriac حܢܣ, perspicuus, honoured, excellent (in *J. Th. St.* xxxiv, 1933, p. 39).

xliii 22. you rejected me. Cf. Zech. iii 2, יגע ב, the opposite of בחר ב.

xliii 25. I do not remember your sins. The meaning is: I do not realize your sins. *ẕkr* means: to make the influence felt, be operative. See Johs PEDERSEN, *Israel its life and culture*, Copenhagen 1926, I/II, p. 106f. The verb to sin presents more than the pure act of rebellion. The verb includes both the rebellious act and its after-effects, the punishment.

xliii 27. your interpreters. The intercessors repeat— ליץ — the words in an understandable form. The ancestor will be Jacob, mentioned as a sinner likewise in Hos. xii 3ff. H. N. RICHARDSON translates "your spokesmen", *V.T.* v, 1955, p. 168.

xliii 28. Read וָאֲחַלֵּל and וָאֶתְּנָה.

xliv 5. another shall call himself. I read יְקָרֵא.

xliv 8. And there is no rock without my knowledge. I read בְּלִי דַעְתִּי, unaware. The text can be rendered too by: I know not any. Rock is metaphorical language for God.

xliv 11. devotees, committed to the idol. The stem חבר means: to tie, oblige, being bound in religious duties. Cf. xlvii 9.

xliv 12. if. גם, also, means too: if, in case of. Cf. xlvi 7.

xliv 13. sitting in a house. Or, to dwell in a house, presenting a family deity.

xliv 16. I feel (the fire). The verb ראה indicates a wider conception than the action of the eyes. It means: to receive impressions, e.g. perceiving sounds, death; being hungry, being sleepy, feeling warmth, fear, pleasure, seeing future and life.

xliv 21. these things. Our verse is no direct continuation of vv. 9-20, but it links up with vv. 1-8. The vv. 9-20 are a unity without a stringent connexion with their context. They depict the worthlessness of wooden idols. In verse 21 are *these things* Yhwh's deeds.

xliv 23. is glorified. Yhwh has adorned himself by redeeming Israel. This conception starts from the covenant idea. Yhwh's divine character manifests itself in his people. Yhwh and his people constitute a unity.

xliv 24. who was with me, K·tib. The meaning is: nobody was with me ,I alone was ordering the world, and likewise I alone am deciding Jerusalem's future. Jerusalem is at present a chaos but it will be a rebuilt town before long. The meaning of *K·tib* does not distinguish widely from that of *Q·re*, by myself.

xliv 28. he shall fulfil. Cf. verse 26. Perhaps *K·tib* יַשְׁלִם, he shall restore, make complete.

xlv 8. so that salvation and privilege are fruitful. The verb פרה means to be fruitful. Subject of this verb in plural can only be ישע וצדקה, salvation and right, privilege. צדקה presents a "heilbringende Faktor" (K. Hj. FAHLGREN, *ṣ·daḳa, nahestehende und entgegengesetzte Begriffe im A.T.*, Uppsala 1932, p. 79f.), a granted right, given by God, see ROSENTHAL, *a.c.* Subject of the next verb, תצמיח, is again the earth, the subject of תפתח.

all at once, see ad xl 5.

xlv 14. the result of labour. I.e. the acquired property, result of toil, parallel to the commercial benefit of Kush etc. The enumeration of Egypt, Kush, Saba is not fortuitous. The names of these countries will have caused a clear idea of might and riches. But even those mighty and rich peoples, slave-owners *par excellence*, will become subjected to you, O

Israel!, is Second-Isaiah's message. Israel, himself a slave of rulers in former days and at present, will be the owner of those who are proverbial slave-owners. With this figure of speech Second-Isaiah underlines the reality of Judah's forth-coming liberation. We need not pay any more attention to the foreign peoples here mentioned than this figure of speech necessitates. They are mentioned *ad maiorem gloriam dei judaici* in order to strengthen the weak faith of the exiles.

xlv 19. in vain. Adverbial, cf. xlix 4.

xlv 24. trustworthiness. In conformity with verse 23. צדקות mean at the same time the firmness and the good results of Yhwh's deeds. His grants, shown in the salvation are his ornament, his glory, cf. xlvi 13. They contrast with the vanity, the chaos, תהו. The rebuilt town and temple are token both of Yhwh's victorious strength and of the renewed covenant.

he comes to him. I.e. Yhwh comes to Israel, his people, among which many are incensed against him.

xlvi 1. Their idols become beast and cattle. After the exclamation: the bending Gods, Bel and Nebo!, follows the depiction of the beasts of burden. היה ל means to become, to serve as.

your things lifted up, carried, is an attempt to render the terse style of the Hebrew text literally. The meaning will be: you, people of Bel and Nebo, as a burden. The conception of God as the carrier of his people is continued here and in the following lines. A God wo is unable to bear his people presents himself as worthless.

xlvi 3f. Jacob's house and Israel's remnants are Yhwh's burden. In evident contrast to Bel and Nebo is Yhwh able to bear his people from the womb to the grave. Such a divine carrier is a real saviour. Cf. Is. lxiii 9; Ex. xix 4; Numb. xi 12; Deut. i 31; xxxii 11.

xlvi 4. Since I have made, I will both bear etc. The three Imperfects are dependent on the Perfect "I have made", עשיתי.

xlvi 7. If. Cf. verse 11*bis.*

xlvi 10. my counsel, my decision. See the writer's "The Counsellor" in *Wisdom in Israel and in the Ancient Near East,* Suppl. to *VT,* Vol. III, Leiden 1955, p. 42ff.

xlvi 11. the man of his counsel. K·tib. The third person will be caused by the standard expression.

xlvii 2. strip off your robe. The taking off one's upper garment means setting oneself to (slave-)work. G. R. DRIVER translates: strip off the train, in "Difficult words in the Hebrew Prophets", *Studies in O.T. Prophecy,* Edinburgh 1950, p. 58.

xlvii 3. I will not come upon a man. The meaning of the verb פגע is to meet, come upon. Coming upon no man means that nobody prevents him from taking vengeance. The virgin Babylonit appears to have not any defender and this figure of speech shows evidently her hopeless situation.

xlvii 5. stiffening. I suggest a stem *damam,* to be stricken dumb, be petrified by fear in דּוּמָם. See the writer's article on Is. xxxviii 9-20 in *OTS* ix, 1951, p. 178f.

mistress of kingdoms. גברת is she who gives orders, who decides as a ruler.

xlvii 7. a lasting ruler. One who decides concerning the future, see the writer's *The Counsellor,* a.c.p. 58: ruler of the future, sure of her position while she possesses the strength to determine coming events. This idea of continuation through domination of the future is, in my opinion, the right sense of עד.

realize, or, remember. See ad xliii 25.

xlvii 8 and 10. no one besides me. See ad xliii 11.

xlvii 9. incantations. Cf. for the stem חבר xliv 11.

xlvii 11. that you do not know, unprecedented.

xlviii 1. Listen. I. e. come in the ban, the closed circle with its own rules and privileges; follow the wake of the speaker.

the waters, i.e. semen virile, Targum.

remember, i.e. realizing Yhwh as a living God, using his name in your oaths.

xlviii 8. inconstant. Or, changeable. The stem בגד means: to break a contract, to dissolve a covenant, change over from one party to another. The breaking of a covenant is of course condemned by the party left alone. The usual translation in our dictionaries is derived from this unfavourable aspect of the verb: to act treacherously. But the original meaning of the stem is neutral. See the writer's remarks on Ex. xxi 7-11 in *Orientalia neerlandica*, Leiden 1948, p. 165f.

xlviii 10. not to get silver. Refining-works produce fine silver, but Israel's refinement is not done because of its own value, only because of Yhwh who had associated his name with this people.

xlviii 11. My lustre I do not give to another. This expression does not point to Yhwh's faithfulness to his people or to his love and forgivingness, but to his zeal not to lose, to waste his lustre once connected with this people. Yhwh's shine, lustre, consists of the welfare of his people. See on this bold but faithful statement of Second-Isaiah chapter VI, p. 116.

xlviii 14. and his arm [against the] Chaldeans. I prefer this rendering to the reading of the Septuagint, "and the seed of the Chaldeans", because of the suffix, *his* arm. Similar to Yhwh's purpose Yhwh's arm means his might, which will be realized against the Chaldeans by Cyrus. The rendering, however, remains uncertain.

xlviii 16. and his spirit. It seems to me possible that this words mean that Second-Isaiah considers himself as the interpreter of the happenings inspired by Yhwh's spirit.

xlviii 21. This verse is in conformity with xli 18ff, xliii 19ff; xliv 3. They realize the traditions concerning the exodus from Egypt and explain herewith, in Second-Isaiah's opinion, the happenings of his time as Yhwh's wonderful salvation of the Judeans.

xlviii 22 = lvii 21. Probably a liturgical addition.

xlix 3. O Israel. There are no grounds for omission. See J. A. BEWER on the textcritical value of Kenn. 96 in "Two Notes on Is. 49, 1-6" in *Jewish Studies in Memory of G. A. Kohut*, New York 1935, p. 86ff., and once more in his contribution to the *Festschrift für A. Bertholet*, Tübingen 1950, p. 67. The word Israel is certainly fatal to any individualistic theory.

xlix 4. disintegration. The reverse of consolidation. His labour is without the effect that is aimed at, his wages are not paid out.

xlix 5. that Israel be not swept away. There exist two meanings of the Nif. of אסף *a)* be gathered—if taken here the negation לא must be altered into לו, thus *Q·re*—; *b)* disappear, fade away, taken away. If this meaning is taken the Masoretic text לא must be retained.

xlix 6 f. See chapter V, p. 94ff.

xlix 8. to bundle up. I.e. to integrate, making a whole, a covenant; the renovation of the former state. See chapter V p. 94.

xlix 20. draw close together. The verb נש means: to force up, push up, send up. Cf. Gen. xix 9.

xlix 21. What about these? Cf. Judg. viii 18.

xlix 24. a conqueror, victor. Cf. xli 2.

l 2. in distress. See G. R. DRIVER, *J. Th. St.* xxxi, 1930, p. 276f. Cf. too Ugar. *b'š*, to be bad.

l 4. to speak fluently. The colourless rendering of the Septuagint, εἰπεῖν, has caused an emendation of לעות into לענות; and the rendering of the Targum, לאלפא, has caused the fantastic supposition of reading לרעות, from which the rulership of the servant is deduced! I think that we have here the stem לעה (לעע), Arabic لغا, to speak excessively, abundantly, inconsiderately, rashly.

li 1ff. See chapter III, p. 58ff.

li 4. for instructions go forth from me and my judgement for a light to peoples. This line indicates the clearness of the judgement that is manifest to everyone. The scale of clearness is expressed by the surrounding world, the peoples who will see and respect what Yhwh has done. See further chapter V, p. 92.

li 5. my salvation goes forth. I am not convinced that these words are a gloss on "my grant (victory, deliverance as privilege) is near". Grant (right) and salvation namely occur often together. Cf. verse 6.

li 6. in like manner. Another rendering is "like locusts", see J. REIDER, "Contributions to the Hebrew Lexicon" in *ZAW* liii, 1935, p. 270f.

li 19. who will comfort you? The Masoretic text reads: "how may I comfort you?". I take the position of those who emend the text, reading יְנַחֲמֵךְ, in order to get similarity with the interrogative sentence "who is moved with regard to you?". I suggest the possibility that we may suppose here an original reading מיא instead of מי, and that this 'alef may have caused the Masoretic reading אנחמך.

li 23. Bow down. See G. R. DRIVER, *J. Th. St.* xxxi, 1930, p. 280, who refers to the Akkadian stem *šiḫû*, to descend, sink down. DRIVER translates: roll (on the ground).

lii 1. beautiful (garments). Or, ornamental (garments), token of strength and welfare.

lii 4. at the last. This rendering suits, I think, better than the usual: for nothing. Vv. 3 and 5 express the latter idea, using the term חִנָּם. At the last is in agreement with at first in the first part of the sentence.

lii 5. What about me. I prefer K·tib to the Masoretic מַה לִּי. The meaning of the expression is very clear in Naomi's question to Ruth, Ruth iii 16, מִי־אַתְּ "How did you fare?".

lii 6. shall know my name. I. e. shall know by experience how I reveal myself, how I work.

Here I am. This is the standard expression in a conversation to wit the start of a talk. He who uses this expression gives to understand that he is prepared to deal with the affairs brought to him by the other. He says: I am considerate.

lii 7. rules. Literary: is king. Cf. D. MICHEL, *V.T.* vi, 1956, p. 52ff.

lii 8. eye to eye. I.e. before their eyes. Cf. Numb. xiv 14; Jerem. xxxii 4.

lii 13ff; liii 1ff., 4, 8f, 9, 11. See chapter VI, p. 102 ff.

liii 10. When he has made atonement. I suggest a reading אִם תָּ(א)שֵׂם אָשָׁם נַפְשׁוֹ. M's reading שִׂים אָשָׁם occurs only here.

liii 11. his rest. This is a tentative translation. I assume in דעת the second stem ידע, become still, quiet, at rest; the Arabic ودع ; discovered in some places of the Hebrew Bible by D. WINTON THOMAS, *J. Th. St.* xxxvii, 1938ff.

He shall see. The verb ראה is used here absolutely. The meaning is: he shall live prosperously, in peace. The addition אור, light—cf. already the Septuagint and also the DSIa text— may be called a right explanation of the Masoretic text. Be satisfied with rest can be depicted by "the man sitting under his vine and under his fig tree", none shall make him afraid.

my righteous servant shall acquire privileges. Privileges, granted by God, guaranteeing a renewed life in peace.

liii 12. laying himself bare. I.e. carrying his life in his hands, without the least reserve, unconditionally prepared to self-renunciation.

holding up. The verb נשא means: to lift up, bear. With regard to sins the meaning is not to forgive but to hold up that the sequel, the normal sequence of evil deeds, cannot be realized. Punishment does not come over the evildoers. Cf.

the writer's monograph „De Voorbede in het Oude Testament", *O.T.S.* iii, 1943, p. 53ff.

liv 4. expel nations, and *people desolate cities*. These expressions are figures of speech illustrating the numerousness of the people, at present in straitened circumstances but before long to be delivered and rising greatly.

liv 7. For a brief moment. A rendering in conformity with verse 8. Another rendering is: "with little emotion" (DRIVER, *J. Th. St.* xxxvi, 1935, p. 299).

liv 9. like Noah's days. כִּי־מֵי considered as כְּמֵי = כִּי־מֵי, "like the waters of" seems to me unnecessary. כִּי־מֵי > כִּימֵי "like the days of", is preferable because of the comparison of periods which will be meant here.

liv 15. over my head. אָפֵס מֵאוֹתִי, without my knowledge.

lv 4. Yhwh's devotion has been shown in David's prosperity.

lv 5. The renewed people will be instead of a slave of foreign rulers a strong, commanding people, respected by everyone, like Israel in David's time.

This unexpected turn makes the redeemed nation a witness of Yhwh's might for the nations. Even unknown peoples will be impressed by this wonderful salvation of a weak and scattered group of men. This is a figure of speech to emphasize the greatness of the deliverance. See further chapter V, p. 90ff.

lv 8. plans. Including the execution of the plans. The verb חשב means too both planning and execution, to reckon, charge, cf. a.o. Mic. ii 1; 1 Sam. xviii 25; 2 Sam. xix 20; Lev. xvii 4.

lv 12. the mountains, the hills and the trees of the field. Together the whole country of Palestine. The mountains, hills and the trees are joyful, they sing and clap their hands. This is a metaphor, picturing the fertility and the richness of fruit, cf. Ps. lxv 13f.

lv 13. a name,—an everlasting token. Yhwh's name is Yhwh's work. His mighty deeds are the redemption of the exiles, the reconsilidation and the renovation of the Judean people. "This is the heritage of the servants of Yhwh", זאת נחלת עבדי יהוה, liv 17. *Monumentum aere perennius.*

THIRD CHAPTER

THE ROCK

A note on *Q·re* and *K·tib* of Isaiah li 1

The usual translation of the first verse of Is. li runs "Hearken to me, ye that follow after righteousness, ye that seek the Lord: look unto the rock whence ye were hewn, and to the hole of the pit whence ye were digged".

There are no variants of importance to the Hebrew text of the Masorah. The *Q·re ḫuṣṣabtem* and *nuqqartem*, Puʿal or passive Qal forms, corresponds with the ancient and modern versions which, for elucidation, add "from which", ἐξ ἧς, ἐξ οὖ (Lucian); ὅθεν, ὅθεν (Symmachus); ἐξ ἧς, ὅθεν (Theodotion); ܚܠܣܘ (Peshitto); מן (Targum); *unde* and *de qua* (Vulgate). Only the oldest Greek version, the Septuagint, differs from the passive reading of the Masorah by rendering the active aorist, ἣν ἐλατομήσατε, ὃν ὠρύξατε, "Look to the rock *that you have hewn* or, *that you hew out*, and to the hole of the pit *that you have dug* or, *that you dig*".

In our Grammars the passive construction of the Masoretic reading is explained as an old passive of Qal, see a.o. BAUER und LEANDER [1]), referring to studies of BÖTTCHER and BARTH. And the construction of the sentence which needs some addition in our renderings is explained as a double elleptic relative subordinate clause [2]).

In Jewish tradition there are some traces of the interpreta-

---

1) *Historische Grammatik*, Halle 1918ff, p. 287.
2) ED. KÖNIG, *Historisch-komparative Syntax der hebräischen Sprache*, Leipzig, 1897, par. 380c.

tion shown by nearly all the ancient versions and the *Q·re* of
the Masoretes, wherein the line: "Look to the rock" has been
explained with the beginning of verse 2, "Look to Abraham",
thus taking the word "rock" as a methapor for Abraham.
R. Hanina bar Pappai, a rabbi of the third generation of the
Amorim, 3rd and 4th cent. of our era, explains the rock in
Deut. xxxii 30, "How should one chase a thousand, and two
put ten thousand to flight, unless their rock had sold them,
and the Lord had given them up?", with our passage from
Isaiah. He sayed: צור, rock, means Abraham, according to
Is. li 1. The same text from Deuteronomy is in the midraš—
the midraš Exodus rabba li 7— evidence that the exile was
Abraham's choice as punishment for his descendants who
became unfaithful.

The understanding of Abraham as the rock, means that
the rock in our passage is a metaphor for infertility, and
analogous to this, the understanding of Sarah as the quarry,
means that the quarry, the cavern too is a metaphor for
sterility. R. Ami, a contemporary of Diocletian, also of the
third generation of the Amorim, quotes our text, saying that
Abraham and Sarah were persons whose genitals are hidden,
or, undeveloped, טומטומין, b. Yamut 64a.

In the midraš Esther rabba vii 10 r. Jose ben Lakunya
compares the Israelites with boulders, referring to Balaam's
blessing out of Numb. xxiii 9 and our text, Is. li 1.

In ancient and in modern interpretations we find the same
idea. The Portuguese Dominican FOREIRO states in his
commentary [3]) on verse 2, "Look to Abraham" etc.: "expli-
cat, more Scripturae, quod obscurius dixerat". CALVIN,
translating "petram excisionis" and "cavernam cisternae",
writes: "The origin of the Jews is compared with a rock and

---

3) Venice 1563, Antwerp 1565.

a cavern, and the Jews themselves with the stones cut out. According to the following sentence Abraham and Sarah are compared with a quarry, a stone-pit". This commentator calls it "a strange metaphorical language". In commentaries and translations of more recent days I did not find a divergent meaning. There is only, as far as I know, a slight variant rendering, the rock *from which* you were hewn, and, the rock *where* you were hewn [4]).

This passive reading, *huṣṣabtem, nuqqartem*, handed down in the Masoretic text and for the sake of clearness rendered with an addition *from which*, is generally accepted in almost the whole history of biblical interpretation. It is possible that as early as the first century of our era one knew already the above stated interpretation. I recall the Gospel text: "God is able from these stones to raise up children to Abraham", Matth. iii 9, Luke iii 8.

In some studies on our passage some notion of the difficulties in the Masoretic tradition can be read. CALVIN spoke, as we saw, of a strange metaphorical language, and FOREIRO admitted that the expression in verse 1 is obscure. In recent books on Isaiah I did not find any objection to the usual interpretation. The idea of Abraham and Sarah, the ancestors of the people, rendered by a rock and a stone-pit from which the stones are hewn, seems to cause no trouble for them. We find several explanations of the metaphor Abraham= the rock. The most simple opinion is that of Maimonides: the rock means the origin. This meaning can be found too in Deut. xxxii 18, "You were unmindful of the rock that bore you and you forgot the God who gave you birth". The rock, however, is here a metaphor of Yhwh. Other opinions are: Abraham is called a rock because of his unshakable faith. Or,

---

4) The latter rendering in B. DUHM's commentary, Göttingen, 3rd ed. 1914, p. 354.

because of his and Sarah's deadness of life, see Paul in Romans
iv 19, "He did not weaken in faith when he considered his
own body, which was as good as dead because he was about
a hundred years old, or when he considered the barrenness of
Sarah's womb." The rock is then similar to the wilderness of
verse 3, the ruins of Zion.

There remain, however, some serious difficulties with
regard to the Masoretic reading of the text as well as with regard to the true meaning of the metaphor. If we should
suppose a passive reading of the verbs used in the text we
must add at any rate מִמֶּנּוּ, or מֵאֲשֶׁר. This very construction we
have found in almost all the ancient versions. But a supposition of a passive reading is far from probable. The consonantal
text suggests an active sentence, חֲצַבְתֶּם and נְקַרְתֶּם, "Look to
the rock that you hew out and to the hole, the cistern, that
you dig". This is the reading of the Septuagint. The Qᵉre
of the Masoretes seems to be made for the sake of the interpretation of the passage with the equalization of the rock
and the pit with Abraham and Sarah.

Before we turn our thoughts toward this equalization I
wish to dwell on the meaning of the terms used. The verb חצב
occurs almost exclusively in Qal-forms [5]). A Puʿal or a passive
Qal does not occur except in the reading of the Masoretes
in our verse. חצב means "to hew out". That which is hewn
out is mentioned in the accusative. Mentioned are *cisterns*,
e. g. "They have forsaken me the fountain— מקור — of living
waters, and hewed out cisterns for themselves —חָצְבוּ לָהֶם בֹּארוֹת—
broken cisterns, that can hold no water". (Jerem. ii 13). Compare further Deut. viii 9; Neh. ix 25; 2 Chron. xxvi 10. Then

---

5) Deut. vi 11; viii 9; 2 Reg. xii 13; Is. x 15; xxii 16; Jerem. ii 13;
Ps. xxix 7; Prov. ix 1; Esra iii 7; Neh. ix 25; 1 Chron. xxii 2, 15; 2 Chron.
ii 1, 17; xxiv 12; xxvi 10.
Once we find a Nifʿal, Job xix 24; and once a Hifʿil, Is. li 9.

a tomb, "What have you to do here and and whom have you
here, that you have hewn here a tomb—כִּי־חָצַבְתָּ לְּךָ פֹּה קָבֶר,
you who hew a tomb on the height—חֹצְבִי מָרוֹם קִבְרוֹ—, and
carve a habitation for yourself in the rock?", (Is. xxii 16).
Further *pillars*, "Wisdom has built her house, she has hewn
her seven pillars—חצבה עמודיה שבעה—", (Prov. ix 1; G., S.,
Tg. set up.). Then *copper*, "—a land in which you will eat
bread without scarcity, in which you will lack nothing, a
land whose stones are iron, and out of whose hills you can
dig copper—ומהרריה תחצב נחשת—", (Deut. viii 9, recording
the qualities of the land into which Yhwh brings his people.)
The material which is hewn is also in the accusative. "The
stone-cutters"—חצבי האבן (2 Reg. xii 13; 1 Chron. xxii 15).
אבן is used parallel to צור, rock, in Gen. xlix 24, אבן ישראל.

The verb נקר is seldom used in the Hebrew Bible. It means
in Qal "to bore, pick, dig", and occurs in 1 Sam. xi 2; Prov.
xxx 17 with the eyes as object; in Pi'el too with the same object
in Numb. xvi 14; Judg. xvi 21 and Job xxx 17, meaning "to bore
out". These are all the places where the verb occurs other than
our verse in Is. li 1 with its Pu'al or passive Qal reading.

The stem נקר has an important derivative, נְקָרָה "hole, cleft,
cavern". "And while my lustre passes by", reads Exod.
xxxiii 22, "I will put you in a cavern (a cleft) of the rock—
נקרת הצור— and I will cover you with my hand until I have
passed by". And in Is. ii 21 we read: "to enter the caverns of
the rock and the clefts of the cliffs — לבוא בנקרות הצרים
ובסעפי הסלעים—from before the terror of Yhwh, and from the
glory of his majesty, when he rises to terrify the earth". In
both places we have to do with caverns wherein one can find
a hiding-place in times of danger.

מַקֶּבֶת is formed from the stem נקב, "to pierce". In four
places [6] מקבת is a tool by means of which one drives in nails
_____
6) Judg. iv 21; 1 Reg. vi 7; Is. xliv 12 and Jerem. x 4.

and pegs [7]). In our verse מקבת means the place where one pierces, the hole, the result of piercing [8]).

The Siloam inscription includes some words which illustrate the meaning of the expressions under consideration. We read in line 1: . . . . the boring through. And this was the story of the boring through . . . דבר · היה · זה · הנקבה. הנקבה·בעוד. In line 2: and whilst yet there were three cubits to be bored [through, there was hear]d the voice of each calling . . . ·להנקוב. And in lines 3 and 4: And on the day of the boring through the stone-hewers struck . . . ·הכו · הנקבה · ובים. החצבם. The lines 3 and 6 mention the rock, הצר. Line 6: . . . the height of the rock above the head of the stone-hewers.

This description of an incident in the boring of the tunnel contains the stem נקב, to bore, a substantive נקבה, the boring through, the term חצבם, stone-cutters, and הצר, the rock. Ben Sira, in his passage on Hezekiah [9]), records the same event: . . . and he hewed through the rocks with iron and dammed up the pool with mountains—ויחצב כנחשת צורים ויחסום הרים מקוה.

The second word, בור, perhaps a gloss for elucidation, means a cistern, hewn in the rock to keep the collected water. I refer to "the cisterns hewn out which you did not hew" from the enumeration of the qualities of the country in Deut. vi 11 [10]). Illustrative too, are two lines of the Meša stone 24f: "And there was no cistern —בר— in the midst of the

---

7) BROWN, DRIVER, BRIGGS; KÖHLER suggests a second stem נקב in מקבת, hammer.

8) Compare the derivatives נֶקֶב, hole, cavity (ALBRIGHT: mine, BASOR 110, followed by KÖHLER, Lexicon); and pass; נְקֵבָה, perforata female.

9) xlviii 17.

10) Cf. Neh. ix 25 and 2 Chron. xxvi 10.

city, in Qrhh; and I said to all the people, Make you each a cistern — בר — in his house".

The water supply is one of the most important things in the life of man and every settlement is dependent on the possession of wells and cisterns. It is a special token of Yhwh's grace that the Hebrews found the cisterns hewn out when they took possession of the country. In this context belongs the term the rock with its clefts and cisterns, wells and caverns. Even the rock in the wilderness is water-bearing, Exod. xvii 6 (the Horeb); Deut. viii 15; Pss. lxxviii 20; cv 41; cxiv 8; and in our chapters of the Book of Isaiah xlviii 21. Besides water as life-giving strength provided by the rock the honey from the rock with which Yhwh will satisfy his people is mentioned, Ps. lxxxi 17.

It is from here, in my opinion, that we must try to interpret the metaphorical use of the term rock. The meaning of rock in metaphorical language is nowhere "place of wilderness, desert". Rock is on the contrary everywhere a name of Israel's God and the context in which this name for Yhwh is used does not contain any notion of his devasting power or of his unapproachableness. The rock is God as the protector and provider of life and security. "O Yhwh, my rock and protector" — צוּרִי וְגֹאֲלִי — (Ps. xix 15); "They remembered that God was their rock, that God most high was their protector" (Ps. lxxviii 35) [11]). And Second-Isaiah himself uses the metaphor in like manner: "Fear not nor be afraid; did not I tell you from of old and did not I report? You are my witnesses, are you not? Is there a God besides me? And there is no rock of which I am unaware" (xliv 8).

The rock is a manifestation of Israel's God. Yhwh is "the rock in whom I take refuge", Ps xviii 3. There is no

---

11) Cf. A. R. JOHNSON, "The primary meaning of √גאל" in *Suppl. to VT*, Vol. I, Leiden 1953, p. 67ff.

trace in the Hebrew Bible that Abraham was mentioned with the metaphorical name rock, neither in a sense of unfruitful barrenness nor in a sense of firmness or refuge. It is Yhwh himself who gives protection and life, who guarantees the future of his people. He and he alone is the rock. A guardian character or stability of the rock is, as far as I see, not stressed in the metaphor. The main idea seems to be the rock as a hiding-place, refuge and source of life, the rock as water-bearing, being a rock with caves and cisterns.

Those who pursue rights, who seek Yhwh, are parallel to those who hew out the rock, who dig the cistern or pit in Is. li 1. Yhwh's rights, his privileges granted to his believers, his oracles, decisions that guarantee the future of his people, are life-giving and protecting qualities. People who apply to the provider of grants, the protector of life are depicted in the second line of our verse as people who hew out the rock to find the life-giving water, who dig a cistern that can hold water, or who dig a hiding-place in the rock, a refuge in their God, in Yhwh. Yhwh is Israel's horn of salvation, his water-bearing rock, his hiding-place and refuge. In opposition to this are the Gods who have no real strength to save their worshippers. People who trust them are like men who hew out cisterns that cannot hold water, broken cisterns. In time of disaster they do not help, they cannot renew the life of the people, they are worthless. To worship Yhwh means to put your confidence in a life-giving God.

Is this interpretation of verse 1 in agreement with the context, vv. 1-3, and does it fit in with the main trend of Second-Isaiah's ideas? The sense of the passage is: Yhwh reminds, by mouth of his messenger, the exiles of his wonderful and life-giving strength. The banished people are desolate and without hope. But now Yhwh will show his gracious and mighty power like he has done in former days, building his nation from Abraham and Sarah. His lifegiving strength will bring life from death: the ruins of Jerusalem, the wilderness of Judah will be changed into a joyful place, a garden of Eden. Those who are unbelieving must look to the wonderful origin of the people: the birth of a nation from the ancestors, Abraham and Sarah, both old and childless when Yhwh called them. Second-Isaiah found in the story of the ancestors his argument and illustration for his message. His aim is to recall the true character of Judah's God. Yhwh is Judah's rock. Yhwh is Judah's well. They dig the well, is said of the covenanters of Damascus [12]), they who dig the well of many waters are Yhwh's true believers.

This interpretation is, as far as I see, in keeping with the meaning of the Hebrew ideas of the text as well as with the main trend of Second-Isaiah's preaching. The passage in Is. li forms a strong unity, describing Yhwh's strength. Abraham and Sarah are but a manifestation of this strength, an instance, an illustrative instance of Yhwh's wonderful power. Abraham is no rock at all and the Israelites are no stones hewn out of a rock, no figures sculptured from a rock. It is Yhwh himself who is the real centre of the passage. In conformity with the main trend of our chapters it is Yhwh who blesses his people again, renewing their life after a period of disaster and death.

In this way we are rid of the difficult and unusual reading *ḥuṣṣabtem* and *nuqqartem*, the *Qᵉre* of the Masoretes. We must read the active form, the frequently attested Qal, *ḥᵃṣabtem* and *nᵉqartem*.

There still remains the question: why did the Jews alter the sense of our passage? They did not add consonants or words to the text. When they gave their *Qᵉre*, the passive reading of the verbs, there must have been a fixed text, in their opinion

---

12) Zadokite fragments, ed. SCHECHTER, p. 3, l. 16; p. 6, l. 3f; in reference to the song of the well, Numb. xxi 18.

immutable, "holy". Otherwise they would have added *mimmènnu* and *mimmènna*, or, *me'°šer*.

Their alteration shows a great respect to Abraham, their father. He receives in their reading of the "holy" consonants a title which is otherwise only used for Yhwh himself: the rock. I think that the Masoretic reading is one of the instances of the growing veneration of the Patriarch and the patriarchal stories in Judaism.

It seems to me not impossible that in the final period of the Old Testament times and in the post biblical period there has been some hesitation to use the metaphor: hewing out in the rock, digging the pit, for "seeking Yhwh", taking refuge with him. However that may be, the similarity in the expressions: look to the rock, and look to Abraham, may have facilitated the introduction of a new reading. Hebrew was no longer spoken language and this may have weakened the feeling for the language. Moreover the reading of almost all the translations does not give an obtrusive feeling because they have added *from which* (you are hewn etc.). It puzzles me, however, that, in spite of the difficult and unusual reading of the Masoretic *Q•re*, and in spite of the otherwise often quickly used version of the Septuagint, in our modern translations and interpretations I did not find any trace of doubt on the reliability of the Masoretic tradition. I hope to have shown that there is reason to break a lance for *K•tib*.

THE TRADITION OF THE TEXT

It may have struck the reader of the translation and the notes in the first three chapters of this study that I did not mention the Isaiah scrolls from the Judean desert. Since the texts of these scrolls have been available the matter of their contributions to textual criticism has been the centre of interest. A stream of studies has come down from this pinnacle of the discoveries in our field. And many of them offer readings of the Isaiah scrolls (DSIa and DSIb, the latter to a lesser extent) as corrections of the Masoretic text. Recently, however, there is more reserve with regard to the superiority of the reading of these manuscripts. Our knowledge of the earliest known history of the Hebrew manuscripts and of those of the ancient versions indicates a multiformity which makes a correction of one manuscript by means of variant readings in another or in retranslated versions very doubtful. Besides, our insight into the complex character of the Masoretic text is enlarged. Nevertheless, my reader has a right to know why I am reticent concerning a reconstruction of the Masoretic text with the help of variant readings in the Isaiah scrolls. I will therefore deal once more with the places wherein I depart from the Masoretic text with special regard to the DSI. Further I will make some remarks on some variant readings adopted by other students of these texts. And in conclusion I will treat some characteristic features of DSIa.

The translation of Is. xl-lv, presented in chapter I, does not number many cases wherein I deviate from the Masoretic text. In *xli 2* I suppose a scribal error, at once corrected, or, a reading יְלֹד, see the interpretative note in chapter II. The pointing of the three letters יְלֹד is an attempt to wring from them some sense. DSIa tries the same, reading יוריד. The scribe of DSIa makes his copy readable by means of adding *matres lectionis*. It is not easy to gather from his reading a system of pronunciation. At any rate is certain that his pronunciation differs from that fixed in the punctuation of the Masoretes. Cf. above all the reading of the suffixes. But DSIa's scribe added more letters. So he added to the first word of verse 3 a *waw*, reading וירדפם and this addition bars the way to the solution of the crux suggested above.

In *xli 25* I accept LE CLERC's emendation (from the seventeenth century), reading ויבס. But my arguments differ from those used by him and his followers. Neither the scrolls nor the ancient versions support this correction.

In *xlii 20* DSIa is equivalent to M, reading the third person.

In *li 19* I read with DSIa and the ancient versions the third person, ינחמך. M. H. GOTTSTEIN observes [1]: „Das alle Übersetzungen so lesen beweist wenig". I agree with this observation. I found different grounds for the emendation, see chapter II.

xl 10. The alteration of the vowels in בְּחָזָק into בְּחָזֵק, generally accepted, agrees with DSIa's *plene* writing and with the rendering of the ancient versions. It is, however, a sound principle that the cause of the incorrect reading must be clear before the emendation may be accepted. Neither the variant reading nor the ancient renderings inform us on this point. The Masoretic punctuation preserves not seldom a double tradition [2]). It seems to me possible that M's reading

---

1) In "Die Jesaia-Rolle im Lichte von Peschitta und Targum", in *Biblica* 1954, p. 69.

2) Cf. a.o. O. H. BOSTRÖM, *Alternative Readings in the Hebrew of the*

in its vowels retains a variant reading, see chapter II, p. 41.

In *liii 9* a contraction of two words can be supposed, see chapter VI, p. 114. DSIa reads here בומתו, an instance of the many inaccuracies of the copyist, whose manuscript arouses now and then doubts of his knowledge even of Hebrew.

The other cases where I deviate from M's reading are all a preference to *K·tib*. The places are *xlii 20a*; *xliv 24*; *xlvi 11*; *li 1*; *lii 5*. In xlii 20a in agreement with DSIa and the ancient versions. In xliv 24 in agreement with DSIa, מיא אתי. The Septuagint has a different division of the sentences and takes the words under discussion as the beginning of verse 25, rendering τίς ἕτερος. S, Tg and V consider the term as a parallel to לְבַדִּי, alone. Their renderings are: "alone—by myself", "by my Memra—by my might", "solus—et nullus mecum". In xlvi 11 I retain the third person, עצתו, in agreement with DSIa. S and V read *Q·re* of the Masoretic text, G offers a free, explaining version, περὶ ὧν βεβούλευμαι, and Tg departs far from the text by rendering: "the sons of Abraham, my chosen". The arguments of my preference of *K·tib* to *Q·re* in li 1 are set forth in chapter III. My reading is in agreement with the Septuagint. DSIa reads חצבתמה and נקרתמה, giving no indication whether a passive or an active reading is meant. In Is. i 6 a *waw* is inserted, to mark the passive reading, but in xxxii 14 (and in xiv 3?) no *mater lectionis* is used. In lii 5 I prefer *K·tib*, contrary to DSIa. The scroll reads מה, M's *Q·re* מִי, a specimen of the phonetical character of its spelling.

There are more variant readings in DSIa and some of them are already adopted in translations and interpretations of our part of the Bible [3]). Millar BURROWS, whose portion in

Books of Samuel, Rock Islands, Ill., 1918, and the present writer's researches into the text of 1 Samuel, Amsterdam 1938 and Leiden (*OTS*) 1942 and 1949.

3) O. EISSFELDT's list of the variants, Stuttgart 1951, is far from complete. GOTTSTEIN's additional list, published in *Biblica* 1953, and

editing and studying of the scrolls from the Judean desert is
considerable great, treats in his book on the Dead Sea
Scrolls [4]) the thirteen variant readings of DSIa adopted in the
Revised Standard Version [5]). The growth of the reserve with
regard to the superiority of the manuscript's readings appears
from his uncertainty about the value of some of these thirteen
emendations by means of the Isaiah scroll. ". . . in some cases,"
writes BURROWS [6]), ". . . I am now convinced that . . . the
Masoretic reading should have been retained".

I will dwell now on the places from Is xl-lv which are
emended in the Revised Standard Version (abbreviated as
RSV). xlv 8 is rendered in RSV

    Shower, O heavens, from above,

       and let the skies rain down righteousness;

      let the earth open, that salvation may sprout forth . . .

Instead of M's ויפרו DSIa reads ויפרח. BURROWS observes:
"The difference is not important; either reading is quite
possible, and the choice between them is hardly more than
a matter of subjective preference [7])". There is, however, more
subjective preference in RSV's rendering of this verse than is
granted in this observation. There are in the same verse five
other variant readings in DSIa not adopted by the translators.
The variants are: הרועו instead of M's הרעיפו ; ממעלה instead
of ממעל ; ויזל instead of יְזֹלוּ ; האמר לארץ instead of תִּפְתַּח־אֶרֶץ ;
and the omission of M's last line יַחַד אֲנִי יהוה בְּרָאתִיו .

LÖWINGER's "New corrections to the Variae lectiones of O. Eissfeldt",
published in *VT* 1954, are valuable but not complete. LÖWINGER
published too the variants of DSIb, in *VT* 1954. Of great importance
are GOTTSTEIN's studies, "Die Jesaia-Rolle im Lichte von Peschitta und
Targum", and "Die Jesaiah-Rolle und das Problem der hebräischen
Bibelhandschriften", both in *Biblica* 1954.

4) *The Dead Sea Scrolls*, New York 1955.
5) New York 1952.
6) *O.c.*, p. 305.
7) *O.c.*, p. 309.

Our verse is a good specimen to put some questions of more than casual importance. Why is only one of the six variant readings adopted and why specially the fifth of the series? I wonder whether a satisfactory answer can be given. A reconstruction of the so-called original form of the text by means of variant readings selected on subjective grounds is in my opinion open to question. The same applies to an arbitrary use of the ancient versions in reconstructing the Hebrew text. Each manuscript and each version must be valued after a determination of its characteristic features before any opinion can be formed concerning its worth to reconstruct the traditional text. Every increase of our knowledge concerning manuscripts and versions enlarges at the same time the multiformity of the texts and their history. This state of affairs does not allow us to speak of an *original* text. An arbitrary use of variant readings brings us from the field of textual criticism into the field of conjectural emendation. And here BURROW's advice holds good: "The only adequate protection against . . . unwarranted emendations is the combined judgment of competent, conservative, and at the same time open-minded scholars" [8]).

In chapter II, p. 49 I have tried to determine the significance of the Masoretic reading. It is no more than an attempt and certainly no decision about an original reading. In my opinion M's complicated text is more understandable than DSIa's obscure reading.

In xlv 2 RSV reads

> I will go before you
> and level the mountains.

Instead of M's הֲדוּרִים DSIa reads הררים, cf. G: ὄρη; DSIb הרורים, or, הרירים. The plural הרים is used in post-biblical

---

8) *O.c.*, p. 303.

Hebrew. DSIb is as usual closer to M's reading than DSIa. A transposition of the letter *reš* into the letter *dalet* is an easier supposition than a clerical error הדורים instead of הררים. Therefore I prefer the Masoretic reading.

In xlix 24 RSV reads

> Can the prey be taken from the mighty,
>
> or the captives of a tyrant be rescued?

DSIa reads עריץ instead of M's צַדִּיק. This reconstruction is in agreement with a supposed parallelism in verse 24 and verse 25. Cf. too G, S and V. עָרִיץ is used in verse 25 as a synonym of גִּבּוֹר. M's reading, a righteous man, i.e. a man whose success is evident, a privileged man, a conqueror, makes, however, good sense. And an alteration of עריץ into צדיק seems to be more difficult to conceive than a co-ordination with the terms used in the next verse.

li 19 has been dealt with above, p. 69.

In xlix 5 DSIa reads לו instead of M's *K·tib* לא. DSIa reads the meaning: "to be gathered" in the Nif. of אסף. The suggestion that M's reading לא was introduced in opposition to the Samaritans depends on the improbability that the Masoretes the Samaritans identified with Israel. Instead of עֻזִּי, my strength, DSIa reads עֶזְרִי, my help, a weakening of the sentence, like Tg's explanation.

The pronouncement of בניך, xlix 17, in M בָּנָיִךְ, your sons, as בוֹניך, your builders, seems to me in spite of the rendering of some versions and the reading of DSIa no improvement. They who come to the town, verse 18, are Jerusalem's sons, the sons of her bereavement, verse 20, who will all gather and come to the town as her ornament. If we read the passage as a unity the term "your sons" suits much better than the term "your builders".

DSIa differs in many cases from the Masoretic text. In order to obtain an idea of the nature of these differences I deal with a number of verses chosen from each of our sixteen chapters. I select those verses that offer readings with a difference of meaning as well as readings differing in spelling and pronunciation only.

xl 11. Two cases of *plene* writing: כרועה and בזרועו. Addition of ה in ובחיקוה. The '*alef* of M's טלאים is lacking. In this case the letter '*alef* does not belong to the stem, טלה. The same holds for the spelling in DSIa of גי, xl 4; מזנים, xl 12, 15. It is obvious to consider these readings as better than M's spelling with an '*alef*. DSIa's use of the letter '*alef*, however, is in such a manner variable and shows often Aramaic influence that its correct spelling in our cases may be by accident. אבד is spelled without '*alef*, xli 11; ברא, *idem*, xlii 5; xlv 6; liv 16; קרא, *idem*, xlii 6; xlv 3; xlvi 11; xlviii 13; li 2; liv 5; שאף, *idem*, xlii 14; נשא, *idem* xlix 22; באש, *idem*, l 2; כתוא, *idem*, li 20; צואר, *idem*, lii 2; טמא, *idem*, lii 11; ראש, *idem* xl 21. ראשן, *idem*, xli 4, 27; xliii 9, 18, 27; xliv 6; xlvi 9. On the other hand the spelling ראשית, רואש is found, xlvi 10; li 11. And ראשן with '*alef*, xlviii 3, 12, 16; lii 4. And קרא, xlviii 15; lv 6; cf. the additions or corrections, קרא in li 19; lii 12; and of ברא, in li 6; liv 16. Remarkable too is the spelling of בראוש with an '*alef*, xli 19 and lv 13; and of שפאים, xli 18; xlix 9. See further the last paragraph of this chapter.

The spelling עולות instead of M's עֹלֹות, the participle of the verb to suck, may be a plural of עוּל, a sucking (child), once used in M, xlix 15.

xli 11. The first word, הן, is added above the line. Two cases of *plene* writing, יבושו and כול. The spelling of the suffixes, בכה, M's בָּךְ; and ריבכה, M's רִיבֵךְ. The spelling of יובדו, without '*alef*, see *ad* xl 11. Omission of two words: יִהְיוּ כְאַיִן. These words occur too in verse 12 and are probably overlooked in our verse.

xlii 22. Addition of the letter *hê* in והואה. *Plene* writing in

כולם, הוחבאו and אומר. M's מִשְׁסֶה is read as למשוסה (9), similar to M's *K•tib* in verse 24. Cf. Tg and S, לְבִזָּא. Remarkable is the *dot* under the letter *yod* in בחורים.

xlii 24 and xliii 21. DSIa reads זה instead of M's poetic pronoun זו. xliii 21. Addition of a *waw copulativum*, and (my praise). ויאמרו, a colourless substitute of M's יְסַפֵּרוּ, written *plene*.

xliv 16. Supralinear addition of ועל, adding a *waw*. The added *waw* before וחציו is not removed in spite of the corrective addition. M's participle, יֹאכֵל, is altered into ויאכל, in agreement with the following verbs of M. The reading ועל גחליו ישב, "and he is sitting above his coals", instead of the continuation of the idea of taking food, may be a misreading of the copyist, connected with the alteration of אַף, in M indicating a new idea, into *waw*. The secondary character of the alteration appears perhaps too from the spelling ישב, contrary to the usual *plene* writing. ויואמר, *plene*. The significance of the verb ראה in this context is probably not discerned, DSIa reads נגד.

xlv 20. Four cases of *plene* writing: לוא, ובואו bis, and הנושאים. As usual הגואים is spelled with an '*alef*. The *hê* after פסלמה seems to be added afterwards, being the *mêm* written as a final letter. Cf. the same in xli 16; xliv 18; lii 3, 11. No final *mêm* is found, on the contrary, in xlii 19; xliv 5; xlv 4; xlvii 9; xlviii 1; xlix 8, 18, 24, 26; l 2 and li 3. Instead of M's יַחְדָּו DSIa reads ואתיו, probably a mistake וְאִתָּיו (וְאִתּוֹ).

xlvi 10. Three *plene* writings: מראישית, לוא and וכול. The spelling of מראישית with '*alef* I have already noted. אחרות would be a scribal error [10]). The reading of the third person, יעשה, instead of the first, is perhaps caused by the suff. 3rd pers. "his counsel" in verse 11.

---

9) Burrows, *The Dead Sea Scrolls of St. Mark's Monastery*, New Haven 1950, reads למשיסה.

10) Burrows transcribes in his ed. *o.c.* אחרית.

xlvii 5. Three cases of *plene* writing: וּבֹאוּ, בחושך and לוא. Further the spelling כשדיים as in verse 1 and xlviii 14, 20; *kî* with a final '*alef*; and the reading גבורת, superiority of (?). דממה may be a reminiscense of 1 Kings xix 12. See chapter II, p. 51.

xlviii 14. DSIa reads Imperfects: "They assembled all of them and they listened"—"and he has reported", יקבצו כולם ויגיד; וישמעו. The reading of the 1st pers.(suff.) אוהבי is probably in agreement with the reading "my purpose", חפצי [11]), instead of חפצו. But זרועו, written *plene*, but without *waw copulativum*, has the 3rd pers. (suff.). וישה will be a scribal error, omission of the letter ע.

xlix 18. The spelling סאי is post-biblical Hebrew. כולם and נואם [12]) are written *plene*. לכי, no pausa-form. כיא with a final '*alef*. Remarkable is the *dot* above the letter ש in תלבשׁי [13]).

l 6. Two cases of *plene* writing: לוא and ורוק. Instead of "those who pull out the beard" DSIa reads "those who throw (stones)", מטלים and instead of the verb "to hide" DSIa reads the verb "to turn aside", סור. Both variant readings give a suitable sense. There are as far as I see no grounds to use these readings as emendations of M's text.

li 2 and 3. DSIa produces here too the differences characteristic of the manuscript, the writing *plene*, the suffixes *-kemah*, *-temah* etc., the final '*alef* in כיא, a *yod* added as *mater lectionis*. Besides we find instead of the stem ברך, M's "I blessed him", a form of the stem פרה, "I made him fertile". This difference seems to be caused by the standard combination פרה and רבה in the Hif., to make fruitful and make many. Further we find an addition in verse 3, taken from verse 11, "sorrow

---

11) Burrows transcribes in his ed. *o.c.* חפצ.

12) In xli 14 נאום.

13) Other cases of dots (except as corrective mark) are xlii 22, quoted above; xlix 8 (?); li 11 ופזורי "and the scattered...".

and sighing shall flee away", an expression already known from Is. xxxv 11.

lii 12. Four cases of *plene* writing: לוא bis; הולך, and אלוהי. Further twice *kî* with final *'alef*; ובמנוסא with an Aramaic ending; and twice the suffix *-kemah*. And an addition, אלוהי כול הארץ יקרא, taken from liv 5, reading יקרא, with *'alef* as M, in contrary to DSIa in liv 5 where יקרה is read.

liii 12. פושעים is written *plene*. The final letter of נמנא is corrected in a *hê.* והואה, usual writing. Instead of M's singular חֵטְא־ a plural is read, חטאי, in agreement with the collective meaning, cf. G, S and Tg. Instead of the Hif. of M, יַפְגִּיעַ ל ? "he made intercession for", DSIa reads the Qal, יפגע ל ?. In post-biblical Hebrew the Qal means to entreat (Yhwh), to beseech; or, to attack. Instead of M's פֹּשְׁעִים, the rebels, sinners, DSIa reads, פשעיהמה their sins, their rebellious deeds. Cf. G. It is possible that DSIa's reading has the same meaning as the Syriac version: he attacked their sins; S: he attacked the sinners. But the interceding character of action of the servant can also be meant: he made intercession for their sins.

liv 11. Three cases of *plene* writing: אנוכי, לוא and ויסותיך. The last word is a superlinear correction of ויסודו. Instead of M's סערה, being in commotion, a synonym is used in DSIa, סחורה, going around.

lv 12. כיא, as usual with a final *'alef.* רונה, instead of M's רֻנָּה, as usual in DSIa. וכול, *plene.* Instead of M's תּוּבָלוּן, "you shall be led forth", DSIa reads תלכו, "you shall go", a less colour-full expression. *-kemah*, instead of M's *-kèm* in לפניכמה. And ימחא instead of M's יִמְחָאוּ, probably a scribal error.

The frequent use of the letter א is one of the most puzzling features of the scrolls from the Judean desert. On p. 74 I have already shown that DSIa is not consistent in its writing. Even our small part of the scrolls, not quite 14 columns, includes

enough cases and varieties to convince us of the complication
of this orthographical phenomenon.

Besides the cases of an unsystematic use of the letter 'alef
enumerated on p. 74, the irregularity of DSIa's spelling can
be demonstrated by the following words: מיא, 14 times in
our sixteen chapters, and מי, also 14 times; ליא, 7 times, and
לי 10 times; ביא, 3 times, and בי, once; כיא, more than 75
times, and כי, 4 times; עואר and עור, xlii 19. Peculiar are the
spellings עמיא, li 16, lii 6; קצאוות, xli 5, however, קצוות in xl 28;
אולם, xli 7; אפוא xlii 25; אדס, lv 13. The ending ־֫יֶ֫ is spelled
יהא־, xl 2, 22; xli 9; xlii 5 etc., but not always, cf. חטאותיה, xl 2;
וצאצאיה, xlv 12. Aramaic influence may have caused the
readings נרצא, xl 2; מוזנים, xl 12, 15; מרוש, xl 21; אקשיבו, li 4;
רבא, li 10; מנוסא, lii 12; שמעוא, liv 2.

For obvious reasons the pronunciation of the generally
used spelling כיא has engaged the students of the scrolls.
GUILLAUME [14]) and BARDTKE [15]) have proposed the reading
kî'a. BARTHÉLEMY [16]) thinks that the reading kî'a would have
been written as הואה with a final hê and not with an 'alef. He
thinks that the final 'alef preserves the reading kî, precluding
the misreading kaî, cf. Zakkai and such-like.

The spelling of the words ציאה, xli 18, and עואר, xlii 19;
xliii 8, are possibly illustrative for the use of the letter 'alef.
The letter is used at the end of a syllable and seems to mark
the readings -wā (or ,-wē) and -yā, giving the preceding letter
a consonantal character. The full vowel of the preceding
letter is indicated by the 'alef in readings like נאים, cf. the
Aramaic spelling עאני = עֲנִי in the Targum.

There remain several questions and problems concerning

---

14) In *Revue biblique*, 1952, p. 184f.
15) *Die Handschriftenfunde am Toten Meer*, Berlin 1952, p. 65.
16) In *RB* 1953, p. 455.

the scrolls with Biblical texts, difficult to understand. I hope to have made clear in the preceding remarks on several variant readings why no direct use is made of them to reconstruct the Masoretic text. It is still too early to determine exactly the significance of these texts for our knowledge of the Biblical times.

FIFTH CHAPTER

THE LIMITS OF SECOND-ISAIAH'S MESSAGE

No one can boast of having read all the books and articles written on the conceptions of Second-Isaiah. C. R. NORTH [1]) as well as H. H. ROWLEY [2]) have recently surveyed in an excellent manner a great number of studies, and they have obliged all of us by this. I confine myself to some studies, representing I think the main ideas of scholarship on the subject of this chapter. My purpose is not to discuss every argument used. I refer to them mainly in order to introduce the question of the limits of Second-Isaiah's message. Even a short reference will enable us to discern the textual base of the conceptions.

As mission of Yhwh's servant ROWLEY [3]) states: "—to lead the nations to God.—Israel was called to a mission to the world,—that mission was the corollary to her election by the only God to be His people. No prophet lays greater emphasis on the election of Israel; no prophet stresses more clearly the doctrine of monotheism. If God is the only God, then His worship is for all men; and if He has chosen one people to receive His revelation, then it is for her to share it with all. The conception of Israel as the Servant, charged with a mission to bring all men to the true religion, is there-

---

1) *The Suffering Servant in Deutero-Isaiah*, Oxford 1948.

2) *The Servant of the Lord, and other essays on the Old Testament*, London 1952. The two contributions on Second-Isaiah in it are of 1950.

3) Earlier studies of ROWLEY on the same subject are *Israel's Mission to the World*, 1939; *The missionary message of the Old Testament*, 1945; *The rediscovery of the O.T.*, 1945; *The Biblical doctrine of Election*, 1950.

fore intimately related to other elements of teaching of this prophet".

The subject election has been treated recently too by Th. C. VRIEZEN [4]). He writes: „Wir wissen was der Auftrag des Knechtes Gottes, des *bachir* Israel, in Jes. 42: 1-4; 5-9 ist: er hat das Recht auf Erden zu bringen: die Küstenländer warten auf die Tora, die er bringt. Er ist gegeben zur *berith 'am* (Bund des Volkes), zum Licht der Völker". VRIEZEN's interpretation concurs in many aspects with ROWLEY's views. Is. xlii is treated as an unity, without distinction between the first lines, usually taken as a song by itself, and the rest of the chapter. VRIEZEN follows in his interpretation of the servant in this part of the book the collective explanation, in contrast to his idea about the servant in chapters l and lii 14-liii 12. He differs from ROWLEY in his interpretation of the missionary task. He reads iñ Is. xlii 1 ff: Israel ought to go abroad in order to bring *mišpaṭ* „das Recht", to the nations, without violence or force but by the spirit. He uses the term „Weltmission", meaning penetrating of the nations of the world by individual members of the Israelite people [5]). *bᵉrit 'am* is explained as „Bund der Menschheit, oder Völker", covenant of mankind or, of the nations. He refers also to chapter xlix, speaking of the great missionary conception of the Second-Isaiah. He translates the crucial text, xlix 6, as follows: „Zu wenig ehrenvoll dafür dass du mein Knecht bist, ist es, dass man die Stämme Jakobs aufrichtet und die Bewahrten Israels wiederbringt: so mache Ich dich zum Licht der Heiden, dass mein Heil sei bis an der Welt Ende".

The relation of the conception of redemption with the doctrine of creation, the conception of a universal God, has

---

4) *Die Erwählung Israels nach dem Alten Testament*, Zürich 1953, p. 65.
5) *O.c.*, p. 67.

been treated by G. von Rad [6]). The idea that the doctrine of Yhwh's creative power is closely related to and incorporated into the conception of salvation, redemption, has been underlined by many students. RENDTORFF even concludes to a fusion of both doctrines [7]), I refer further but to ZIMMERLI's treatment of the conception of the servant [8]), an article with independent views, which we will mention later in this book. ZIMMERLI rejects the interpretation of the servant as a missionary, a conception difficult to visualize. He lays emphasis on the term *mišpāṭ*, several times used. The task of the servant is proclaiming Yhwh's *mišpāṭ*, a realisation of Israel's right, its internal affairs, material and spiritual. But his task, be it first and foremost a task concerning Israel, is not limited to this people [9]). xlix 5ff „berichtet von einer gewaltigen Ausweitung der Aufgabe des Knechtes, die ihm in einer Stunde sichtbar gemacht wird, in der er am Erfolg seiner Mühen verzagen will". ZIMMERLI refers here also to xlii 1ff. He finds a parallel text in Jeremiah, xii 1-6, where the comfort of the despairing prophet should be the increase of his burden.

BLANK [10]) and MORGENSTERN [11]) read in the frequently used formula "I, Yhwh" the indication of the universal God. He alone is God and there is none else. "I, I (am) Yhwh, and besides me there is no saviour", xliii 11 a.o. In spite

---

6) „Das theologische Problem des alttestamentlichen Schöpfungs-glaubens" in *Werden und Wesen des alten Testaments, BZAW* 66, 1936.
7) R. RENDTORFF in *Zeitschrift für Theologie und Kirche*, 51, 1, 1954.
8) In *Theologisches Wörterbuch zum Neuen Testament*, V, 1953, p. 655ff.
9) *A.c.*, p. 668.
10) In *HUCA* xv, 1940, p. 1ff. E. g. p. 31: "If one considers the message of the literary prophets from Amos through Ezekiel, and if then one turns to the message of Isa. 40-55, one is immediately aware that here a new spirit animates the words — a freer, broader spirit — one which reaches out beyond the borders of Israel".
11) In *JBL* lxii, 1943, p. 269ff.

of this universal character, they say, Yhwh stands none the less in a peculiarly intimate relation to Israel. MORGENSTERN calls it a worldwide choice. Only the One Universal God could make such a choice. Manifestly Deutero-Isaiah affirms, according to this scholar, that primarily He was the Universal God, and only secondarily, as an act of choice by Him and only in order to fulfil His universal purpose, did He enter into a particularistic relation with Israel, more intimate than His relations with other nations, either individually or collectively. This concept, it is clear, is but a corollary to Deutero-Isaiah's basic concept of the Deity as the God of time and history, universal in time as well as in space who, as Creator, was at the very beginning of existence, i.e. before the birth of Israel, and therefore must have been the Universal God first and primarily, long before He called Israel into being and chose it as His people and servant. Thus far MORGENSTERN.

A. NEHER is in his monograph, *L'essence du Prophétisme* [12]), in line with these ideas of MORGENSTERN. He lays special emphasis on the covenant of Yhwh with all mankind. He states: "La *berit* avec Noé—*noahidique*—est la loi de l'humanité.— le serviteur évoqué par Isaïe, comme *lumière des nations* (49,6), et beaucoup de prophéties énoncées par d'autres prophètes ne concernent essentiellement que les *nations*".

And finally, in an article rarely quoted—even ROWLEY does not mention it—of R. MARCUS, "The 'plain meaning' of Isaiah 42. 1-4" [13]), to which I shall refer below, it is stated: "God gives his Servant assurance of support, and inspires him in his task of bringing justice to mankind.—Nothing shall be allowed to prevent him from bringing justice to the nations. He will not falter nor be deterred from bringing justice to the nations, especially because they need his teaching".

12) Paris, 1955, p. 279.
13) In *Harvard Theological Review* xxx, 1937.

There exists a unity in opinion concerning the subject of our chapters: Second-Isaiah does not set any bounds to his message. The servant is elected to receive Yhwh's instructions not only on behalf of the Israelites but also with regard to the nations. The servant, the chosen people is charged with a mission to the world. Yhwh's universality is attended by the missionary character of the elected people.

There are of course shades in the opinions of the interpreters of Isaiah xl-lv. Differences and varieties in interpretation are not at all rare. It is the more notable that we find a virtual unanimity of opinion about universalism in the conception of God and the task of Yhwh's servant. I know but one exception, N. H. SNAITH, whose article [14] will be discussed when I deal with the texts upon which the general opinion is based.

There can be no doubt that Is. xl-lv contains several passages describing the greatness and might of God as orderer of heaven and earth. I recall to mind lines from the hymn in xl, "he who is stretching out heavens like the cobweb...", "bringing out in proper order their (the celestial bodies) host, calling them all by name, not one is missing because of the greatness of his might and strongness in power". And xliv 24, "Thus says Yhwh, your redeemer, and your form-er from the womb: I am Yhwh, who is making all things, stretching out heavens alone, spreading out the earth, who was with me?" Comp. xlv 18; xlviii 12f. F. M. CROSS has shown in an article [15] dealing with the idea of God's court that many passages in Second-Isaiah have a style belonging to a special category, the divine proclamation delivered by a herald and divine directives to angelic heralds. He calls the

---

14) "The Servant of the Lord in Deutero-Isaiah", in *Studies in Old Testament Prophecy*, Edinburgh 1950, p. 187ff.
15) "The council of Yahweh in Second-Isaiah" in *JNES* xii, 1953, p. 274ff.

opening verses of xl a parade example of this literary form. He and other scholars have an open eye for the hymnical style of the passages under discussion.

If we consider the context of the verses referring to Yhwh's ordering power we are struck by their character as quotation. With regard to Second-Isaiah's special purpose they are but aids and appliances. They do not introduce a new concept of God or a new doctrine. They are secondary, taken from a special category and used for a special aim. No typical Second-Isaianic trait can be derived from them. Second-Isaiah uses this conception of God for his own purpose: to underline the power of Israel's God, of Yhwh. The people spoken to appear to be without faith and without hope that their God Yhwh will show them any helpful strength. Second-Isaiah is proclaiming: our God Yhwh has awakened, he will show himself as in former days as a God of power and strength, able to redeem his people, able to renew the scattered and oppressed people.

His use of these hymnical lines is in line with his use of the wonderful acts of Yhwh handed down in the tradition of the Judean people. Yhwh's deliverance from Egypt, his mighty deeds during the exodus, xliii 16f, "Thus says Yhwh, who gave a way in the sea and a path in the mighty waters, who brought forth chariot and horse, army and warrior, they lie down, they do not rise, they are extinguished, quenched like a wick". The foretelling might of Yhwh is another fact from their history, frequently used by Second-Isaiah to prove the trustworthiness of his message.

It seems to be a matter of fact that Second-Isaiah's aim cannot be determined by describing the ways and means he uses to attain his purpose. These ways and means are not his own creation. The peculiar hymnical style indicates a borrowing from elsewhere, an application of an 'El hymn to

his conception of a powerful Yhwh, redeemer of his people[16]).
The emphasis on the exodus he has in common with other
prophets. And the same can be said of the figures of speech,
the arguments from successful foretelling, the challenge to a
lawsuit, the calling to witnesses.

What then is the proper content of Second-Isaiah's preaching? In the recent happenings, in the fall, imminent or
already begun, of the New-Babylonian government he per-
ceives the mighty arm of his God, of Yhwh, bringing about
the deliverance and renovation of his people, of Israel's rest,
the Judean people.

This interpretation of the happenings of his days appears to
be unbelievable to most of his countrymen, in exile as well
as in the parts of Palestine where Judeans still lived. Most of
them had lost their faith in Yhwh, God of the deliverance
from Egypt, God of the patriarchs, God of their former existence in the Davidic kingdom. They were broken down
through the devastation of Jerusalem and its temple of Yhwh,
the devastation too of Judah's cities and through the dispersion of the people. Disaster may be a punishment but abso-
lute and definitive ruination of city, country and people
means the end of Yhwh's meddling with his people, the end
of Yhwh's realm as well.

In this situation of decay, apostasy and dejection sound
Second-Isaiah's word: Yhwh has begun a new work for his
people. He takes action again. He is once more judge and
ruler. And his judgement means a new future for his people,
a future of peace and welfare. He is our redeemer and we,
now despised and disregarded by the nations, we, slaves of
rulers, we will be renewed, our country will be rebuilt, and
we will be respected by everyone!

---

16) This does not mean that such a hymn is not wholly taken in
into Second-Isaiah's religious conceptions.

For this interpretation of the happenings a world-wide conception of Yhwh's strength is needed. His countrymen have to believe that happenings caused by an unknown foreigner like Cyrus are Yhwh's deeds aiming at their salvation.

Considering this background of Second-Isaiah's preaching we may be able to understand his use of hymns, probably already known to Israel previously, related to ideas in the religions of surrounding peoples, here applied to Yhwhistic faith. We may be able as well to understand his laying stress on Yhwh's control of the whole earth, on his continuing dominion. I cannot agree with MORGENSTERN's view that the election, the redemption of the people, is but a corollary of the conception of the deity as God of time and history and creation. I think on the contrary that the idea of redemption is primarily. "Besides me there is no saviour", xliii 11.

A missionary character, "the corollaries of the election", does not appear from the above wording of Second-Isaiah's purpose. The basis for a universalistic missionary task of his central figure, the servant of Yhwh, is supposed to be found in the following passages: the so-called first song of the servant, xlii 1-4 together with the next five verses; the so-called second song, xlix 1-6, also together with its continuation, vv. 7ff; and the passages li 4, 5 and lv 3-5. Some argument too is derived from expressions like the coastlands; heavens and earth; the end(s) of the earth.

The usual translation of these passages no doubt leads to the idea of a world-wide missionary task. I quote some crucial verses: "—he shall bring forth judgement to the Gentiles", xlii 1; "—he shall bring forth judgement in truth (or, reading *la'ummôt*, to the peoples)", xlii 3; "He shall not fail (or, burn dimly) nor be discouraged (or, bruised) till he has set judgement in the earth; and the isles (or, coastlands) shall wait for his law", xlii 4; "—I will give thee for a covenant of the people, for a light of the Gentiles", xlii 6; "And now saith the Lord that formed me from the womb to be his servant, to bring Jacob again to him, and that Israel be gathered unto him (another reading is, but Israel is not gathered, yet shall I be etc.)—for I am honourable in the eyes of the Lord, and my God is become my strength—: yea, he saith, It is too light a thing that thou shouldest be my servant to raise up the tribes of Jacob, and to restore the preserved of Israel: I will also give thee for a light to the Gentiles, that thou mayest be my salvation (or, that my salvation may be) unto the end of the earth", xlix 5, 6; — I will give thee for a covenant of the people", xlix 8; "—I will make my judgement to rest for a light of the peoples. My righteousness is near, my salvation is gone forth, and mine arms shall judge the peoples; the isles (or, coastlands) shall wait for me, and on mine arm shall they trust", li 4, 5; "Behold, I have given him for a witness to the peoples, a leader (or, prince) and commander to the peoples", lv 4.

The conclusion drawn from the passages thus translated is evident. Yhwh's law and peace have to be brought to the nations all over the world. If this conclusion is right we must speak of a world-wide missionary task of Yhwh's servant.

Missionary sense supposes a positive attitude to the nations. Their behaviour and character may be bad and objectionable to this day but they will have a prosperous future, "waiting for Yhwh's law", presented with Yhwh's light. If the usual interpretation is right we are anxious to learn the attitude of Second-Isaiah to the foreign nations and their future.

With regard to this question no conclusion can be drawn from lines of hymnical character, glorifying God's sublimity and transcendency: "—all the nations are as nothing before him", xl 17; "he who is bringing princes to nought", xl 23. Their context shows evidently that these utterances are used with a view to laying emphasis on the greatness of God. But there are other places.

The nations shall be put to shame, foretells xli 11f, and they shall be as nothing. Jacob does not need to fear, he shall be made a sharp threshing sledge, reducing to dust all them who are against him.

Egypt and Ethiopia and Saba are mentioned, in xliii 3, as Israel's ransom given in exchange for the people. SNAITH [17]) is in my opinion right, commenting on xliii 1-7 thus: "This piece tells of God's saving work on behalf of exiled Jacob-Israel. He will give other peoples in exchange for them. There is no universalism here". But I do not agree with his statement that the prophet's interest is not only in the redemption of exiled Israel but also in Israel's exaltation at the head of the Gentiles. Egypt's, Ethiopia's and Saba's wealth shall be gained by Israel, xlv 14. Babel's humiliation and definite fall is theme of the song in xlvii, a song without any sense of mission. Compare further xlvi 1f and li 23; xlviii 14; and xlix 22, 23.

Only the foreigner Cyrus, his successful compaigns, xliv 28, xlv, and probably too xli 1ff, xlviii 14f, are depicted with favourable traits. But neither he nor his people belong to the missionary task of Israel. Cyrus is anointed by Yhwh himself to be his weapon to break in pieces the doors of the prison of his people. Second-Isaiah does not show any further interest in him or in his people.

The expressions "coastlands", "end(s) of the earth", "peoples from afar" [18]) are similar to exclamations as "heavens and earth", "heavens and the depths of the earth", "forest

---

17) *A.c.*, p. 195.
18) xli 1-5; xlii 10f; xliii 9, 20; xlviii 14; xlv 22; xlix 1; xlii 4 and li 5.

and every tree". They are rhetorical words and their meaning is: totality. Everyone is invited to the court of judgement, xli 1, to be a witness of Yhwh's victory. "All the nations gathered together" means to establish the unquestionable evidence and justness of the sentence, the judgement of the court. In some cases the dispersion of the Judean people may be thought of . "Turn to me and be saved, all the ends of the earth", says xlv 22 [19]). The end of the chapter probably gives the interpretation: "—all who are against him shall be ashamed. In Yhwh all Israel's seed shall triumph and glory", xlv 24, 25.

No other conclusion can be drawn from our texts than the statement: Second-Isaiah's only purpose is to proclaim deliverance for the Judean people. "Yhwh bares his holy arm before the eyes of all the nations, and all the ends of the earth see the salvation of our God, lii 10. Foreign nations are but mentioned as peoples to be conquered, in whose hands the cup of wrath will be put, li 23; or as the instrument of Yhwh to deliver his people; or, in rhetorical manner of speaking, to be witness of Yhwh's glory. Yhwh's glory will be shown only in his elected people, raised up from their humiliation.

If the interpretation which reads a world-wide missionary task of the servant in the so-called first and second song of Yhwh's servant and in chapters li and lv is right, we must state that the expressions where upon this interpretation is based are a *corpus alienum* in the book of Second-Isaiah.

Are they an alien element indeed? The servant, acting on behalf of Yhwh—Yhwh puts his spirit upon him, xlii 1— brings forth judgement for the nations. ZIMMERLI is right, in my opinion, when he emphasizes the significance of *mišpāṭ*

---

19) If the whole earth is meant here and not the scattered Jewish people, the emphasis of the sentence remains on Israel's God Yhwh. The Judean country is the only place of salvation.

in our text [20]). It is still better to say, the significance of the expressions הוציא משפט , vv. 1 and 3; שים משפט , v. 4. *mišpāṭ* means a judgement, sentence, a decision given by an authority, a deity, king, priest, wise man or prophet, or given by a court. But not only the sentence, the decision, but at the same time the observing of the regulations, manner or course of life. Judah's manner of life was not hidden from, or disregarded by Yhwh, xl 27. "And all Israel heard of the judgement which the king (Solomon) had judged; and they feared the king, for they saw that the wisdom of God was in him, to do judgement", 1 Kings iii 28. A judgement is much more than finishing a difference of opinion or making up a quarrel. It is a decision about the future, a prescript and determination of the manner of life [21]). Hence its nuances: system of customs and true religion, compare Arabic *dîn*. The word is used parallel to *tora* even in our passage, v. 4. [22])

The servant brings forth, הוציא , and establishes שים , *mišpāṭ*. He makes an end of the controversy and opens a new way of living, giving the judgement and instruction which guarantee a new life. הוציא with the significance "to bring out to" a person or place is usually followed by the preposition אל . There are, however, two places with ל, to wit 1 Kings xvii 13, "bring it forth to me" and 2 Kings x 22, "bring forth vestments for all the worshippers of Baal. And he

---

20) *A.c.*, p. 667.

21) Because of this meaning I do not consider the alteration of לְאֻמָּת (in continuance, a lasting *mišpāṭ*) into לְאֻמֹּת? (for the people) right. Cf. too Second-Isaiah's use of the plural לְאֻמִּים? in xliii 9.

22) J. van der Ploeg, „*šapaṭ* et *mišpāṭ*" in *OTS* ii, 1943, p. 144ff., supposes an evolution from sentence, decision of a judge, to objective religion, „les normes religieuses d'après lesquelles il veut être servi", referring a.o. to Jerem. v 4, parallel to *tora*, "instruction religieuse". Comp. G. Östborn, *Tora in the Old Testament*, Lund 1945, *tora* means "showing the way".

brought them forth vestments". In our place, Is. xlii, the
words "bring forth for the nations" can mean: he brings
judgement out for the nations to receive as their judgement,
their law. But there are some reasons to doubt whether this
is the right meaning of the expression. Firstly, the verb in
Hif'il, הוציא, means frequently: to bring out, cause to appear.
It is used for the appearance of sun, moon and stars, that
Yhwh causes to appear, cf. xl 26. Secondly, the verb with
the sense: to carry to, bring out to or for, is usually followed
by the preposition אל. And thirdly, the nations in Second-
Isaiah are not peoples addressed to by Yhwh or by his servant,
but are mentioned now and then to be witness of Israel's
prosperity after a period of humiliation and slavery.

On the ground of these considerations I prefer an interpretation of our passage in line with the trend of the whole
book. The redeemed people makes appear, shows to the
nations Yhwh's judgement, i.e. their new life from death.
Bringing forth this gracious act of Yhwh means that Yhwh's
work shall be done openly and frankly .This should be a
convincing argument for the desolate people to believe
Second-Isaiah's interpretation of the happenings in the world.
Everyone who sees the redemption of the Judean people, even
great nations, kings and princes, will be astonished and will
respect it as a wonderful salvation. Coastlands, i.e. lands
as far as the end of the earth, will pay close attention to the
instruction given to Israel, an instruction that changes a
people of prisoners into a free nation. The renewed people
will be set as a light, openly seen and respected among the
nations לאור גוים, xlii 6; לאור עמים, li 4.

R. MARCUS[23]) defends with strong arguments the *mašal*
character of xlii 3ab. He takes the verbs as impersonal and

---

23) *A. c.* More or less concurring with C. H. CORNILL, *Der israelitische
Prophetismus*, Strassburg 1894; ed. 1912, p. 139f.

translates: "A crushed reed he may be, but no one shall quench its light; in spite of everything he shall bring justice to the nations". I do not agree with his interpretation of the last line of verse 3 but he would be right in his paraphrase of the first lines. At any rate the servant is here the re-adopted, redeemed people, called by Yhwh to be with his right, privileged by Yhwh. He is made a consolidation of the people, b‧rit ʿam; a light respected by the nations, xlii 6.

The context of these crucial and vexing expressions shows that an undoubted bearing on the Judean people is intended. Verse 7, speaking of opening the eyes that are blind, bringing out prisoners from the dungeon, those who sit in darkness from the prison, is evidently a picture of the dispersed and oppressed people, now on the threshold of liberty. These Judeans will be Yhwh's servant, "Israel", Yhwh's redeemed people, insofar as they believe in and accept the chance of their deliverance. In other words: they become Yhwh's servant if they accept Second-Isaiah's interpretation of the happenings. Yhwh—his name is his honour—does not give his lustre, the effectual side of his relation to his people, to another, xlii 8, comp. xlviii 11. It is evident that foreign nations are out of the question here. Interpreters who start from the idea of a world-wide missionary task of the servant come to very distorted explanations here. "The conversion of the nations", we read in a recent commentary 24), "is here described figuratively. They are now blind, imprisoned and in darkness. They will receive sight, deliverance and light. Although the reference is to the nations, the choice of figures has been influenced by the circumstances of Israel at the moment".

The picture of the Judean people on the threshold of their

---

24) E. J. KISSANE, *The Book of Isaiah*, Vol. ii, Dublin 1943, p. 38.

deliverance is the direct continuation of "and put you to a consolidation of the people, a light respected by the nations", the last line of verse 6. The words describe the position which Yhwh has determined for his people. In xlix 8f our expression —ואתנך לברית עם—occurs in a context which elucidates the real meaning. The passage runs there: "Thus says Yhwh: In a time of favour I answer you, and in a day of salvation I help you, and I keep you and put you to bundle up the people, to erect the land, to apportion the desolate heritages, to say to the prisoners: Come forth! to those who are in darkness: Appear!". bᵉrit ʿam, usual rendered by "covenant of the people" indicates the consolidation of the people after a period of disintegration. PEDERSEN may be right in suggesting in the word ברית an Infinitive of the stem ברי, like בכית, weeping, of בכי; שבית, captivity, of שבי [25]). To make a covenant means to bundle up, to consolidate. Elucidating for this meaning is liv 10 where ברית is used parallel to חסד, devotion, steadfast love. Covenant denotes the unity of Yhwh and his people, guarantee and security for life and welfare of the nation according to the Israelite faith. SNAITH observed rightly [26]) that the servant's mission is limited to his own people. Thus we preserve a unity in the whole passage and our interpretation is in keeping with the main trend of Second-Isaiah's book.

However, there still remains one verse, xlix 6, difficult both to translate and to explain. SNAITH comments this verse as

---

25) *Der Eid bei den Semiten*, Strassburg 1914, pp. 31ff. I do not agree with his translation: „Ich setze dich dazu mit Völkern in *berit* zu treten", explained as „Pflicht- und Friedensverhältnis, Lebensgemeinschaft".

26) *A.c.*, p. 194. He thinks that in xlii 6 לאור גוים — not found in Gᴬ·ᴮ·—is a gloss from xlix 6. The latter he interprets as "a Gentile light", i.e. a world-wide light. The arguments for omission as well as the interpretation of the term in question are not convincing.

follows [27]): "But it is far too small a thing to bring back only all the Babylonian exiles (the tribes of Jacob and the preserved of Israel). The servant's mission is to be 'a light of Gentiles', i.e. a light throughout all the Gentile lands "that my salvation may be to the end of the earth", i.e. my salvation of Israel, since this is the only salvation in which the prophet is interested. The Servant will be a light to guide every Israelite wanderer home. His mission is to gather in all exiles wherever they may be scattered". Although this interpretation contains some right points I do not agree with its tendency. This explanation fails to connect the sentence with its context though the Hebrew text positively indicates such a connection. Moreover SNAITH does not distinguish the construction of the sentence with regard to the subordinate clauses.

SNAITH's explanation, however, differs widely from the traditional commentations. In the commentaries are, of course, differences in details but concerning the main trend they are similar as appears from the following references. DUHM speaks of "der Missionar zwischen Jahve und die Völker [28])". BEGRICH of "die Einbeziehung aller Völker in die Heilsbotschaft des Propheten [29])". EHRLICH paraphrases: "Der Sinn des Ganzen, etwas freier wiedergegeben, ist: um mir als Knecht zu dienen, ist nicht genug, dass du die Stämme Jakobs wiederherstellst, —" [30]). ROWLEY's "election is for service; here: a world-wide service" reflects properly the common opinion, compare finally KISSANE: "The restoration of its (Israel's) national life, which is the object of Israel's hopes and ambitions (5c-f) falls far short of Jahweh's

---

27) *A.c.*, p. 198.
28) B. DUHM, *Das Buch Jesaia*, Göttingen ³1914, p. 342.
29) J. BEGRICH, *Studien zu Deuterojesaja*, BWANT iv 25, Stuttgart 1938, p. 138.
30) A. B. EHRLICH, *Randglossen*, Band iv, Leipzig 1912, *ad loc.*

plan, the true character of which is now revealed"; and: "—
the verse is equivalent to: '*not only* will I restore the national
life of Israel, *but* I will *also* send you to make Me known to
the nations'." [31]).

The ancient versions render our text as follows: G^B καὶ
εἶπέν μοι Μέγα σοί ἐστιν τοῦ κληθῆναί σε παῖδά μου, τοῦ στῆσαι τὰς
φυλὰς Ἰακὼβ καὶ τὴν διασπορὰν τοῦ Ἰσραὴλ ἐπιστρέψαι · ἰδοὺ δέδωκά
σε εἰς διαθήκην γένους, εἰς φῶς ἐθνῶν, τοῦ εἶναί σε εἰς σωτηρίαν ἕως
ἐσχάτου τῆς γῆς. This rendering has more than one interesting
aspect [32]). With regard to our subject μέγα, "great", is a
remarkable translation. The translator seems to have read an
encouragement in our text.

The Targum reads: "and he saith, Do ye regard it a small
thing that ye are called my servants, to raise up the tribes
of Jacob, and to bring back the exiles of Israel? I will also
give thee for a light to the nations, that my salvation may be
unto the ends of the earth". Interesting is the rendering
גלות, the exiles, M's shoots. This translation anticipates
the final words of the verse. Except for the plural rendering,
servants, considering 'ebed to be collective, the Targum is
otherwise a forerunner of the usual translation and interpretation.

The Peshitto reads: "and he saith: a small thing to be for
me a servant and to raise up the tribes of Jacob and to bring
back the shoots—ܢܘܼܒ̈ܠܐ—of Israel. I put you a light for
the peoples in order to be my salvation to the ends of the
earth".

---

31) *O.c.* Vol. ii, p. 128.

32) I refer to I. L. SEELIGMANN, *The Septuagint version of Isaiah*, Leiden
1948. On p. 29 this author deals with the rendering διαθήκη γένους, in
our verse an addition, already known from verse 8 and from xlii 6,
instead of the reading λαός, according to him of Jewish-Hellenistic
origin—the Targum of Esther viii 12—and not of Christian origin—
1 Petr. ii 9, derived from Is. xliii 20. SEELIGMANN does not treat the
initial words of the verse.

There are no variant readings of any importance. DSIa has as usual some cases of words written *plene*, and a different writing of the personal suffix. Further, there is a proleptic suffix in קציו, similar to verse 20; and finally a permutation of the names Jacob and Israel. The differences between the Hebrew text and the Septuagint give no more support to emend the Masorete text.

The main problem of the Hebrew text is the meaning of the expression נקל מן, an expression not without parallels in the Old Testament, but as far as I know not yet convincingly explained. In particular the comparative character of the expression does not appear to full advantage in the usual translations and explanations.

The construction נקל מן is found too in 2 Sam. vi 22 and in Ezek..viii 17. S. R. DRIVER, dealing with the difficult verse in 2 Samuel, states that there are two translations [33]). "And if I play before Yhwh, I count myself still too small for this (to play before him), and am abased in mine own eyes; and with the bondmaids (slave-girls) whom thou hast spoken of, with *them* should I seek (?) to get me honour?", thus runs the first translation. The second one is followed by the modern translators and is also according to DRIVER preferable. It runs: "And I will play before Yhwh, and will be yet more looked down upon than this (more than I have been to-day), and will be abased in mine eyes (or, with G, in *thine* eyes); but with the bondmaids of whom thou hast spoken, with *them* I shall be had in honour".

The usual explanation of this verse is: Michal's taunt that David had degraded himself in the eyes of the bondmaids is unfounded. David says that he might be still more despised by her, and they would nevertheless continue to honour him.

---

33) *Notes on the Hebrew text and the topography of the Books of Samuel,* sec. ed., Oxford 1913, p. 273.

I think that the context requires another translation giving a more exact rendering of the expression נקל מן and a more concrete meaning to David's honour. David's reply to Michal's criticism, —How Israel's king honoured himself to-day, uncovering himself to-day before the eyes of his servants' maids—, starts with a reminder of Yhwh's election of him instead of Michal's father, Saul, verse 21. It is before Yhwh that he has danced. "I will be still more abased (indecent) than this, and I will be dishonoured in my eyes, to wit with the maids of whom you have spoken, with them shall be my honour". David will prefer the female slaves to Michal, Saul's daughter, his wife. Michal's childlessness is the conclusion of the story: "And Michal, Saul's daughter, had no child to the day of her death", verse 23.

Ezekiel viii describes the vision of abominations in Jerusalem and its temple. The usual renderings of verse 17 are in my opinion inexact. The Revised Version reads, "Is it a light thing to the house of Judah that they commit the abominations which they commit here? for they have filled the land with violence—". The revised American Standard Version reads, "Is it too light a thing to the house of Judah that they commit the abominations which they commit here that they should fill the land with violence—". A new Dutch translation [34]) tries to elucidate by adding *not yet* and *also*, similar to KISSANE's attempt quoted above. But these translations do not render the full meaning of the Hebrew expression נקל מן. The accurate rendering must be, I think: "Is there anything more dishonourable (indecent) for Judah's house than committing the abominations which they commit here, for they have filled the land with violence—". This translation respects the 'plain meaning' of the Hebrew text

---

34) A new translation, published by the Dutch Bible Society, Amsterdam 1951.

and is at the same time in keeping with the proper contents of this vision of the prophet.

My translation of Is. xlix 6 is similar to the renderings of the same expression in 2 Sam. vi 22 and Ezek. viii 17. "There is something more dishonourable (indecent) than to be for me a servant, to raise up Jacob's tribes and to bring back Israel's shoots—so that I make you a light to the nations, that my salvation will be (manifest and respected) to the end of the earth—. (7) Thus says Yhwh, Israel's redeemer and separate one, to one despised, to the abomination of the people, to the slave of rulers—: Kings shall regard and princes arise, they shall bow, because of Yhwh, Israel's separate one, who has chosen you".

This is as far as I see a possible translation that takes account of the Hebrew syntax נקל מן. But what is meant by this clause? The meaning seems to be recognizable if we read the passage in connection with its context. The servant, called by Yhwh, is described as fainthearted, verse 4. His situation is very bad, his labour seems to be in vain. But Yhwh encourages him. He says: You think that you are despised, abased, dishonoured, a suffering servant without future. But the tables shall be turned. Your oppressors shall eat their own flesh and be drunk with their own blood as with wine, verse 26; kings and queens shall be your fosterers, verse 23; kings and princes shall bow, verse 7. And you, the despised one, the abomination of the people, the slave of rulers, you shall be respected. Your message, the reintegration of my people, the renewal of my heritage, shall be successfully brought to an end!

The main intent of the passage is: When my redemption shall be fulfilled those who are now the cause of your suffering shall be astonished and full of respect, seeing your prosperity, your salvation. Verse 6 *bcd* are subordinate clauses, indicating in the usual, stereotyped terms the task of the servant of Yhwh, the prophetic program of the open and spectacular renewal of the Judean people. The passage is, in my opinion, an encouragement.

Summarizing we must state that the texts, understood far and wide and from of old as containing a world-wide missionary task of Yhwh's servant, do not allow us to maintain this view. "The so-called universalism of Deutero-Isaiah needs considerable qualification", says SNAITH. Indeed, we can use the term universalism concerning Second-Isaiah's message only if we interpret it quite differently from the usual meaning attached to the word. There is no question of a message, starting from one point and swarming off in the whole world. On the contrary. In Second-Isaiah's message we see all relative to one event. The whole surrounding world, nations, beasts, plants, mountains and hills and depths, heavens and the ends and depths of the earth, relative to the experiences with the exiles. In this manner Second-Isaiah uses his world, describing it as captivated by Yhwh's wonderful deeds: the deliverance of his scattered and oppressed people, the renovation of their existence as a people, the renewing of their country, capital and temple. Life from death.

Besides his environment, terrestrial and cosmic, Second-Isaiah makes use of the creative, ordering picture of the high God, borrowed from elsewhere and already known in hymnical descriptions. And closely related to this he utilizes the history of the Hebrew people, the traditions preserved and interpreted by them for generations. He makes use of everything for his own, special purpose: the interpretation of the happenings of his time as actions of Israel's God to redeem his people. Herewith Second-Isaiah is in line with the spiritual leaders of former days: interpreting events, recent happenings and events to come, comparing them with the past, proclaiming *per analogiam*—the mighty principle of the precedent, *sunna*—the interpretation as decisions of their God, form the function of priest, prophet and wise man.

It is another matter to ask about Second-Isaiah's religious source. SNAITH may be right in his assertion that Is. xl-lv possess a nationalistic and particularistic character. He states[35]: Second-Isaiah is actually responsible for the narrow and exclusive attitude of post-exilic days. But with this not all has been said. Second-Isaiah's interpretation of his time, his application of the events to the adventures of the Judean people, contains a religious view on the relation of Yhwh and his people within the peculiar limits of the Jewish people, but at the same time his interpretation is of a special and unique significance for our approach to the heart of the old Israelite faith. I allude to his conception of the covenant, Yhwh's relation to his people through punishment and suffering. I will deal with this subject in a subsequent chapter.

---

35) *A. c.*, p. 191.

SIXTH CHAPTER

THE SUFFERING SERVANT

The so-called fourth song of the servant, Is. lii 13-liii 12, has often been considered as strikingly different from the rest of Second-Isaiah's book. The picture of the servant is not homogeneous throughout the songs, according to the almost general opinion. ELLIGER has worked out SELLIN's theory that the last song was Trito-Isaiah's work on lexico-graphical grounds [1]). His arguments are examined seriatim by NORTH [2]). It is not my purpose to criticize the many theories about authorship, unity or dissimilarity of the portraits of the servant. My purpose is to see whether the text of the so-called fourth song gives cause to interpret the suffering of the servant as an independent conception, dissimilar to the main trend of Second-Isaiah's preaching.

Our subject is complicated. We are faced with it already in translating xlii 1-4 ."The bruised reed and the dimly burning wick" are considered to be a description of the servant [3]). MARCUS' meaning, however, is further quite different from those who suppose a similarity of reed and servant in order to remove the apparent contradiction between the first and the last song. He explains the portrait of the servant in xlii 1-4 in contrast with the servant of chapter liii. The servant possesses, according to him, an inflexibility and staying-power, in spite of his weakness. He works without an

---

1) *Deutero-Jesaia in seinem Verhältnis zu Trito Jesaia, BZWANT* lxiii, 1933.

2) *O. c.,* p. 81ff.

3) A. o. H. GRESSMANN, *Der Messias,* 1929; SELLIN, *ZAW* lv, 1937; MARCUS, *a. c..*

external sign of power, but with a quiet effectiveness and
without any appealing for help. The suffering of the servant
has been unduly emphasized from the early Christian period
onward, largely because the sublime portrayal of humility
and suffering in chapter liii, which is strikingly different from
most of the book, and which has obscured the predominantly
consolatory and triumphant aspects of the servant as God's
instrument.

It is in line with MARCUS' view that in several treatments of
Old Testament theology Is. liii is considered as a new portrait
of the servant, more or less prepared in some lines of the
preceding chapters but unique in its conception of suffering:
vicarious suffering. L. KöHLER concludes his well-known
description of the theology in the Old Testament in the last
paragraph on salvation through redemption, "Heil durch
Erlösung", with Is. lii 13-liii 12 [4]). I quote some sentences of
this book: „Seine Gestalt ist unansehnlich. Das übrige AT
weiss nichts mehr von ihm. Es ist, als sei er nicht gewesen,
trotzdem er es ist, von dem gesagt wird, dass er Nachwuchs sehe
und an der Erkenntnis Jahwes sich sättige.— Dieser Messias
—wenn man ihn so nennen darf—ist ein Messias, der leidet.
E r i s t e i n M e s s i a s , d e r s t e l l v e r t r e t e n d
l e i d e t . Damit endigt die Theologie des Alten Testaments.

Im Neuen Testament steht die Frage: Verstehst du auch,
was du liesest? Act. 8^{30}".

KöHLER's choice of words is tentative, cautious, more
hinting than claiming to say the last word about it. This
style is in agreement with the uncertainty of the meaning of
the text and the problematical application in the New Testament.

Yhwh's servant in the first three songs, xlii 1-4; xlix 1-6 and

---

4) *Theologie des Alten Testaments*, Tübingen, 1st ed. 1936. The following
references are from p. 229f.

l 4-9, has been characterized as a spiritual hero-figure, endow-
ed with power from Yhwh to act, ready to suffer for God's
cause but by no means a silent sufferer. On the other hand,
the servant in Is. liii is a true martyr-figure, filled with power
from Yhwh to suffer, consumed for others not in that he
labours for them or strives with them but in willing, silent,
vicarious suffering [5]).

NORTH thinks that this difference in portraits does not
mean that there are two servant figures. If so, he says, the
same might be argued from the contrast between the Galilean
ministry of Jesus and His death upon the Cross. He is struck
by the essentially dramatic character of the songs. A dramatist
makes a beginning he may not know to the last detail whither
he is going.

There is some relation between the drama-view and the
individualistic explanation: a drama supposes an individuali-
ty of its principal character. NORTH's opinion, a drama moving
steadily to a climax, makes for the supposition that the servant
is a person not yet appeared but still to come. Along this
line of thought he comes back to what is essentially the traditional messianic interpretation [6]).

Many students of our chapters suppose a certain fluidity in
Second-Isaiah's conception of the servant [7]). They concur
with WHEELER ROBINSON's idea of corporate personality
and his suggestion of expansion and contraction of the servant idea.

Did Second-Isaiah speak of a person to come or of a

---

5) Thus W. STAERK, *Die Ebed Jahweh Lieder in Jesaia 40ff.*, Leipzig
1913.

6) *O. c.*, p. 206f.

7) Besides the studies of NORTH, ROWLEY, VRIEZEN, already quoted, I
refer to A. BENTZEN, *Introduction to the Old Testament*, Copenhagen 2nd
ed. 1952, p. 110ff, and to W. F. ALBRIGHT, *From the Stone Age to Christianity*, Baltimore, 2nd ed., 1946, p. 255.

present servant? If the former is right the songs are myth-provisional or anticipated history, not allegory. LINDBLOM, who published a book on the songs with many original observations [8]), suggests that the songs are allegories, commented in the context by Second-Isaiah. The poems in xlix and l are in his opinion autobiographical allegories, relating historical facts, xlii and liii objective descriptions in the third person, pure fancies. In the fourth song historical and allegorical elements are mingled with each other. LINDBLOM's solution takes full account of the serious questions that proceed from the supposition that the servant in the so-called songs is a person to come. His rejection of the eschatological interpretation seems to me wholly right. "The prophet is conscious that he is witnessing not the end of history, but a new act of a historical drama, which will have its continuation in this world, not in a world to come. The impression of something preternatural and supramundane depends ultimately on his style, on the symbols, comparisons and metaphors which he uses so lavishly. The Second Isaiah is more a poet than a man of doctrine, more a man of an intense and ardent faith than a speculative mythologist [9])".

If the servant is a present person or group represented as an individual it seems possible to take account of the unity of the text, of songs and their context, without the supposition of allegories. The text may be a description of a reality of the past that should be realized again. The people were in former days Yhwh's people, held in his covenant, a people represented by their leaders, charismatic figures, servants of Yhwh, bearing the title of the covenant-sphere. This reality of the past is at present in disorder. The people are in captivity and oppression, scattered and dependent on foreign rulers.

---

8) *The Servant Songs in Deutero-Isaiah*, Lund 1951.
9) *O. c.*, p. 102.

But now they are called to become again what they essentially
have been, Yhwh's people. Behold my servant, behold Jacob,
behold Israel—all ideological names, reminding and magically
realizing the past. These titles are used as a promise and
proclaimed on the ground of a faithful interpretation of the
happenings of Second-Isaiah's time.

NYBERG [10]) and ENGNELL [11]) describe the servant as a
super-individual figure, as a sign given in history, who works
until the present, and will continue to work in the future.
They speak of an oscillation in time, equally typical of this
text with the oscillation between individual and that which
is more than individual. The roots of the servant idea, or
myth as it may frankly be called, are to be found in (*a*) the
Tammuz mystery, (*b*) the ancient Near Eastern kingship
ideology, and (*c*) the conceptions that are gathered round
the tribal ancestor, whose features were both individual and
collective.

The third of the above mentioned roots seems to me the
most important. The Old Testament has plain evidence that
'*ebed Yhwh* has been used as a title of the leaders, the patriarchs
together with Moses, kings and prophets [12]). I am not convinced, however, that we may speak of a myth of a dying
king and his resurrection in our book. The texts give more
cause, I think, to emphasize the special interpretation of real
historical happenings. This typical interpretation is rooted
in the old Israelite faith, realized in an orthodox manner,
illustrated with many poetic images, bringing forth new
things, new faith in Israel's own God Yhwh.

---

10) In *Svensk Exegetisk Årsbok*, 1942, reviewed by NORTH, *o.c.*, p.
220ff.

11) In *SEÅ*, 1945. Comp. too his contribution to the *Bulletin of the
John Rylands Library*, Vol. xxxi, 1948.

12) Cf. C. LINDHAGEN, *The servant motif in the Old Testament*, Uppsala
1950.

Rowley states that it is quite impossible that the concept of the suffering servant was in any sense derived from the contemplation of Israel's suffering in the exile. He is very decided on this point: "The historical sufferings of Israel in the exile can—have nothing whatever to do with the suffering of the Servant [13])". His grounds for this are (a) Israel's sufferings were self-caused by her disloyality to her God, according to the pre-exilic prophets. And Deutero-Isaiah recognizes that Israel has suffered for her sins (xl 2); (b) The servant was suffering not for his sins, but "for our transgressions"—etc. (liii 5ff). This was not the deduction from any historical suffering of Israel, for history knows of none that could sustain it. Rowley thinks that the redeemed people Israel was called to be a light to the Gentiles and that this mission was linked in the person of the suffering servant to an experience of cruel but innocent suffering. Entering into the love—חסד—of God, he says, means at the same time entering into the sorrows of His heart. By her entering into that sorrow Israel could alone hope to fulfil her mission.

This view stands or falls with the traditional universalistic interpretation of the so-called servant songs. Rowley oscillates between a collective and an individual interpretation. In some measure the servant stood for Israel and it equally stood for some individual who should carry the mission of the servant to a unique point. In the fourth song Second-Isaiah seems to be thinking less of a personalization than of a person, according to Rowley. It was in a Person, too, that it found its supreme fulfilment. —Jesus' crucifixion was the consequence of Gods love—the love that loved even when it was rejected [14]).

Zimmerli does not like the idea of a certain fluidity. He

---

13) *The Rediscovery of the Old Testament*, 1945, p. 142.
14) *O. c.*, p. 143.

says of it: "(es) scheint mir nur der Vernebelung der ganzen Fragestellung zu dienen [15])". The suffering of the servant is stated in xlix 7, "the one despised, the abomination of the people, the servant of rulers"; in l 4-9, especially in verse 6, "I give my back to smiters, and my chin to those who pull out the beard. I do not hid my face from shame and spitting"; and in lii 13—liii 12. ZIMMERLI points out the similarity to Jeremiah's suffering. However, in lii 13—liii 12 we do not have a biography, according to ZIMMERLI, but a transcendent picture of the ideal servant, a person to come. Jeremiah's suffering ends in a night without light, cf. Jerem. xx 14ff, "Cursed be the day wherein I was born—". But the servant of Yhwh discovers the signification of his suffering: it is vicarious. This meaning is put into words by the bystanders, interpreted by ZIMMERLI as a crowd of believers ("Schar von Gläubigen"). The suffering servant is not revolting. He knows that he receives right, $mi\check{s}p\hat{a}t$, and reward, $p^{e^c}ull\hat{a}$, xlix 4. His reward is his deliverance from death.

The ancient versions, the earliest chapter of the history of interpretation, show a messianic interpretation of the so-called fourth song. H. HEGEMANN recently has written a valuable book on the renderings of Is. liii in Hexapla, Targum and Peshitta [16]). His purpose is to fix their interpretation and from there to approach the exegesis of liii in the synagogue before Christ. His conclusions are that the ancient versions know a suffering Messiah. The Messiah suffers and dies and his suffering is vicarious, for the sake of Israel, or for the sake of the pious Israelites. He is exalted and made a judge for

---

15) *A. c.*, p. 665ff. ZIMMERLI's opinion is closely related to M. BUBER's *The prophetic Faith*, 1949. BUBER excludes the collective view entirely. The servant is, he says, more than a single human person without, however, having a corporate character. Cf. Ibn Ezra: Israel means an Israelite.

16) *Jesaja 53 in Hexapla, Targum und Peschitta*, Gütersloh 1954.

the impious. These conceptions are very closely related to the New Testament view, without any trace of influence of the New Testament in Aquilla and Theodotion's versions. In Septuagint, Targum and Peshitto we find a similar explanation. There are, of course, differences between them, but generally spoken it may be said that the authoritative interpretation in Jewish circles has been the messianical [17]).

HEGEMANN may be substantial correct that there existed even before Christ a messianic interpretation of Is. lii 13-liii 12 in Jewish circles. He uses strong arguments for a certain similarity both in Jewish and in early Christian circles. Herewith, however, is not decided what the original meaning of the text has been. Both Jewish and Christian interpretations are a part of the history of explanation, the history of Bible use. There are no grounds, in my opinion, to isolate one special part of this history, be it the period of normative Judaism or the period of the early Christian church, in order to give such a part of history a decisive meaning in its Bible interpretation which should stand for every time, before and after this period.

If we give attention to the context of the so-called fourth song of the servant we find in the beginning of chapter lii a repetition of the preceding message. The desolate and despis-

---

17) There is no opportunity here to go into details concerning the relation of exegesis and faith in Judaism. The relation of facts and faith is already an interesting subject in the Old Testament. Cf. a.o. R. H. PFEIFFER's article "Facts and Faith in Biblical History" in *JBL*, 1951. Targum shows many samples of „Umdeutung", alterations, tendentious translations to avoid the personal description of the Messiah as a man of sickness, etc. The discussions of Christians and Jews seem to have caused a re-translation, a tendentious rendering of the Hebrew text in the targum. HEGEMANN, *o. c.*, p. 116ff, summarizes the targumic alterations. NYBERG, *o. c.*, has treated the versions with regard to the Masoretic text. His conclusion is that they are of no help in explaining the Hebrew text. HEGEMANN does not seem to have used the studies of NYBERG, ENGNELL, NORTH a.o.

ed town Jerusalem may put on its ornamental clothes for Yhwh considers the blame of the Judeans as a blasphemy of his name. In other words, Yhwh reminds his people, he realizes the covenant afresh, *de novo*. Jerusalem's ruins shall break forth into singing: "Yhwh bares his holy arm before the eyes of all the nations, and all the ends of the earth see the salvation of our God", lii 10. We saw that this manner of speaking belongs to the typical style of Second-Isaiah who lays emphasis upon the great and unexpected deeds of the lord Yhwh.

The passage known as the fourth servant song is an uninterrupted sequel of the first twelve verses of chapter lii. Yhwh says: My servant, i.e. you people oppressed and partly exiled become now again my covenant-people, redeemed, — my servant shall prosper, he shall be exalted. And everyone, kings and rulers who see it, will be astonished.

After the passage with which we shall deal below, the text goes on with the same conception, liv, lv. The barren one shall have sons, the desolate places of the country shall be overcrowded by a multitude of people. The picture of the people is here very lively. The people in oppression and in exile are portrayed as a forsaken wife, but her lord, *baʿal*, renews the devotion to her, and as in Noah's days after the flood Yhwh swears not to be angry with the people. His salutary covenant shall not totter, liv 1-10 etc.

There cannot be great divergence of opinion about the sense of the context of our passage lii 13-liii 12. I think that those who dissolve the connection of the song and its context take the burden of proof on themselves. An attempt to understand the meaning of the passage in agreement with its context seems to me our first task. I agree with B. D. EERDMANS [18]), O. EISSFELDT [19]), M. BURROWS [20]) and SNAITH [21])

---

18) *De Godsdienst van Israel*, Assen 1930, Vol. ii, p. 43ff; *The Religion of Israel*, Leiden 1947, p. 216f.

that the songs are composed by the author of the surrounding passages, at any rate that they are applied by this author
to his own purpose. The personification of the people is
carried to an exaggerated extent. But the same can be said
of the portrayal of the forsaken wife in liv, an image of the
people as well. Not only do the traits of the portrayal of the
servant as an individual have similarities in texts outside the
songs, but also the idea of suffering is found elsewhere. I
have already referred to the description of the suffering
of the servant in xlix 7, 1 6. It is of some importance, too, to
recall the picture of the barren one, desolate and grieved in
spirit. This portrait of a rejected wife, liv, leaves no shadow
of doubt as to the character of her sufferings. The suffering
of the people is their rejection, reprobation by Yhwh himself.
The outward marks of God's reprobation are the oppression
and the exile, the decay, unravelling like a garment, 1 9,
of the people. It seems to me a matter of sound exegesis to
approach our passage from the main trend of Second-
Isaiah's message.

lii 13 mentions the exaltation of the servant. He is no
longer a slave of rulers (xlix 7), sold by his owner, Yhwh, to
foreigners who treat him badly, but he is redeemed, again
"my servant", Yhwh's servant, the title of the ancestors and
of the leaders, representing the people, later, too, title of the
pious people. This election stated in the opening line of the
passage is a kind of heading which is repeated in the end of
the song, liii 10-12: he shall prosper, he shall divide spoil
with strong men.

The rendering of the verses 14 and 15 of chapter lii is
difficult. My translation is tentative. "As many are astonished

19) *Der Gottesknecht bei Deuterojesaja*, 1933, p. 3.
20) *An Outline of Biblical Theology*, 1946, p. 85.
21) *A. c.*, p. 188.

at you—" (the second person may be a sample of vivid imaginative faculty, henceforth the third person is used) "his appearance is so marred that it is beyond human semblance, and his stature beyond that of mankind—so sprinkled him many nations, and kings purse up their mouths".

The verb נזה means in *Qal*, plus על, to splash, spatter, Lev. vi 20; Is lxiii 3; in *Hif*., plus על, to sprinkle, spray, asperse, Ex. xxix 21 etc. Aaron and his garments, his sons and their garments are sprinkled with blood and the anointing oil, and by that they and their priestly garments are made holy [22]. The sprinkled one is a free man, not longer a slave. The third person singular may be a collective and "many nations" may be a standard expression with collective sense.

The verb קפץ, *ḳapaṣu*, means: to draw together, shut. "Injustice shuts her mouth", Job v 16; "All wickedness 'stops' its mouth", Ps. cvii 42. Kings are accustomed to command [23]. Kings urged to be silent must be an expression for something unheard of, the world turned upside down. From here we can suggest a similar meaning for the first part of the line. "Many nations" are the foreign rulers who do not treat anything as unassailable for them. But in this unheard-of situation impossibilities become a reality: even they respect a former slave. The following line contains just what we expect after this statement: "Indeed, that which has not been told them they see, and that which they have not heard they meet with". The expressions "many nations" and "kings"

---

22) An explanation different from this one is given by VRIEZEN, in *OTS* vii, 1950, "The Term *Hiẓẓa*: Lustration and Consecration", p. 201ff. Cf. for the idea of life-giving by anointment a. o. my „Vive le roi!" in *VT* v, 1955, and an interesting passage in an Akkadian text from Ugarit (shown me by F. R. KRAUS): *aštapak ŠAMNA ana qaqqadiša u uzakkiša*, RS 8.208, 7-9, in "Textes accadiens et hourrites des archives est, ouest et central", Paris 1955, p. 110f, ed. J. NOUGAYROL, *Mission de Ras Shamra*, Tome vi, Le palais royal d'Ugarit.

23) Cf. Job xxix 9, 10, underlining Job's special position.

are probably intentionally chosen by the author. They form a distinct and great contrast to the despised slave. Second-Isaiah's style likes contrasts. If many nations, if kings will be astonished at the servant, there must have been done some wonderful deed which altered his situation totally. In xlv 14 we find the same conception. Foreign nations shall bring their tribute, they shall pass by in chains, they shall bow down to you, they shall pray to you: Only in you is God and there is no other, no God.

Chapter liii starts with *oratio directa*. There are, as far as I see, two renderings possible of the first part of verse 1. We can read, with EHRLICH, "It is unheard, it is unprecedented which we hear"; or we can read the translation given in chapter I of this study : "Who measures up (i.e. answers, comes up) to that which we hear". The second part of the sentence does not cause trouble. The reading is: "and to whom has been revealed Yhwh's arm (i.e. strength)?". שמעה means everywhere: tidings. "Our tidings" means that which we hear, the tidings that we receive.

Verse 1 is an interrogative sentence as often used in Hebrew style to invite, to call forth the reply [24]). This question is put into the mouth of bystanders. These bystanders, too, are speaking in the following verses. Who are they? It is of great importance for the explanation of the chapter to know this. Before I try to give an answer to this question we will read what these bystanders are saying.

In verse 2 לפניו is used parallel to מארץ ציה, out of dry ground. If we do not emend the Hebrew text [25]) and take account of the parallel expression is it perhaps possible to

---

24) Cf. the writer's article on Genesis xxxii in *Ned. Theol. Ts.* 1947.
25) EWALD, in *Die Propheten des alten Bundes*, Stuttgart 1840-41, 3d ed. 1868, reads לפנינו, before us; VOLZ, *Jesaia II*, Leipzig 1932: לא יפה, uncomely. G. R. DRIVER, in *J. Th. St.*, xxxviii, 1937, translates: straight, quoting 1 Sam. v 3, Dagon fallen straight forward.

suggest a meaning: by itself, alone, separated. A young plant alone, without shelter, like a root out of dry ground, the image of an uncovered and vulnerable existence.

The servant is without any attractiveness or charm. He is a man of pains, he does not matter to the bystanders. Nevertheless, אכן, verse 4, they cause his sickness. His bad situation is a chastisement for their transgressions. He carries the after-effects of their bad actions. No one of them is unguilty but they see that the sequel of their guilt strikes him. Nobody has power to withdraw from the after-effects of his deeds. Action and sequel are one. It is Yhwh himself who strikes him with the iniquity (punishment) of them all, verse 6. He is a lonely man and without resistance to his fate [26]).

The use of the first person in the suffix, "my people" in verse 8, and of the name Yhwh, twice in verse 10, shows that the bystanders are no longer speaking, but Second-Isaiah himself. The suffering servant, not redeemed, knows in his disaster death and his grave is with the wicked men. The expression "a rich man", probably meant collectively, is a synonym of the wicked, compare the Book of Psalms wherein the wicked, the rich men are the enemies of the pious people. To be buried together with the impious people was considered a fatal destiny. The pious Judean man wished to be buried "with his fathers", within the family circle. The reading במתיו may be a contraction of two words, בית מתי, Akkadian *bît mutî*, grave, or a corrupt reading of ביתו, "his house", i.e. his grave. The reading "in his deaths" seems to be meaningless.

His very dark fate in slavery is Yhwh's purpose. "Who gave up Jacob as spoil and Israel to robbers? Was it not Yhwh himself, against whom we sinned—?", xlii 24. Indeed, the exile and the dispersion are interpreted by the pious Jews as

---

26) *Fate*, translation of DRIVER, *a.c.* Another rendering is: who of his family (generation) did commiserate (him)?

Yhwh's punishment for the revolts and rebellions of the people. They have understood that it was their God's hand which brought their disaster and they have bowed themselves. But once the time of service came to an end. The period of punishment, however, appears to be longer than they had thought fair. Their time of service became a double time. Hence their dejection.

Second-Isaiah's message is that their suffering, beyond their deserved punishment, was accepted by Yhwh as an atonement for those who remained without punishment. The bystanders of the *oratio directa* in liii 1-6, presented dramatically by the author, may be the part of the Jews who escaped the sad fate of the slaves, Jewish people that found a new life after the disasters of the beginning of the sixth century B.C., be it in Mesopotamia or somewhere in Palestine. I have no definite opinion about the suggestion that Second-Isaiah has used in this passage a liturgy, describing the vicarious suffering of a king or someone else. If so, then he has applied the liturgy wholly to his own purpose.

Chapter liii is, as far as I see, no new element in Second-Isaiah's preaching. His message, *uno tenore*, is derived from an old conception of faith. Yhwh is Israel's God. He gave his name and this means that his function as a God is dependent on the relation, the connection with his people [27]). A God is a

---

27) The names Jacob and Israel, and, too, Jerusalem are used ideologically. They mean to say that Yhwh's people, the people of the covenant is spoken to. Cf. xliv 5, "One shall say: I am Yhwh's; another shall call himself by the name of Jacob; and another shall write on his hand: Belonging to Yhwh; and surname himself by the name Israel." L. Rost seems to me wholly right when he states: „Deuterojesaia — beschränkt den 'Israel-Jakob'-Namen auf die Nachkommen Judas, auf die Judäer. Von Joseph, Ephraim, Samarien ist nirgends die Rede. Der Blick des Propheten ist ganz auf Juda und die jüdische Gola konzentriert. Für sie nimmt er den 'Israel'-Namen in Anspruch". (*Israel bei den Propheten*, Stuttgart 1937, p. 92).

guide, a provider of life in surroundings that every day and every night are full of danger. Rebellion against their own God means decay of the possibilities of living in welfare. The religious leaders speak of transgressions and their after-effects, punishment, oppression, dispersion, exile. But at the same time the covenant is injured. It appears that not only the people is wounded but also their God is offended and wounded. There exists namely a mystical union of Yhwh and his people, *b⋅rît*, covenant. Yhwh chastens and his action is considered as fair and deserved, but this means a punishment for Yhwh himself as well. He is owner of his servant, his people. Exile and oppression by foreigners mean bereavement of his servant. He remains the husband, *ba'al*, of his rejected wife. This is Second-Isaiah's frank starting-point for his faith. I, I am he who blots out your rebellions *for my own sake*"—למעני—, xliii 25. "—it is *for my own sake* that I act", xlviii 11. The master of the sold slave comes back and he redeems his slave, calling him again his servant, "Jacob", "Israel".

Second-Isaiah interprets the happenings of his days from the views sketched above. He goes one step further still. He is aware of an attitude towards life of two kinds. He knows his countrymen, one part by accident or by adroitness having escaped from slavery, one part carrying the hard destiny of a vanquished people. He believes that the proclamation of his comforting faith can be the start of a new, renewed life. The condition is the reconsolidation of the people, becoming again a *b⋅rît 'am*, a covenant.

The suffering for such a long time could not be in vain. Being called in slavery to be Yhwh's servant means receiving new strength to endure the pains of fate, expecting the deliverance. And secondly it means strength to interpret their double suffering as martyrdom, vicarious suffering, inter-

cession for the transgressions who stand in Yhwh's way and
retard the deliverance. Second-Isaiah proclaims the end of
the time of service. The punishment of the people is accepted
as satisfactory, yea as doubly satisfactory, xl 2.

EPILOGUE

Jede Epoche ist unmittelbar zu Gott
LEOPOLD VON RANKE

Nothing is known of Second-Isaiah's personal life. The portrait that can be painted on the basis of his preaching remains sketchy. There are prophetic traits that can be distinguished. He is imbued with Isaiah's ideas concerning Yhwh's holiness. He is familiar with the old custom of applying past history to the present, in order to foretell the future of Yhwh's people. But he does not think in terms of political activity and he does not take action in political life. And this was typical of the prophets in the days of Israel's and Judah's kingdom [1]).

Judah's horizon has been widened through war, disaster and wanderings among the nations. These terrible experiences have been attended by a weakening of belief in their own ability to build up their future. Even activity ordered by their God has become a vague and far-away conception. The dreadful reality of the big powers of their world has swept away their kingship. The consequences have been drastic changes both in political and in spiritual respect. Kingship is the only actualization of national independance in that world, and at the same time the embodiment of religious life and culture. Together with their king their self-confidence has been wiped out.

Hard facts reform even belief. Second-Isaiah's message

---

1) SIDNEY SMITH's characterization of the anonymous man, in his *Isaiah Chapters xl-lv*, The Schweich Lectures of 1940, published in 1944, Londen, p. 75, as a man of the same stature as the first Isaiah seems to me open to discussion.

does not make mention of Judean leaders, judges or kings fighting for the renovation of the scattered and oppressed nation. God no longer entrusts his strength to his agents, the kings of the people. His people's task in the great events of their days—Babylon's fall and Cyrus' rise — is that of the suffering servant. Citizens of small states, willy-nilly involved in the re-division of the world in great communities of interest by the last world war, may be able to some extent to understand the inner transformation of the Judean people in the sixth century B.C. Israel's saving God is a hidden God.

There are also priestly traits in Second-Isaiah's portrait. His preaching seems to be addressed to the congregation and many passages show a spiritual care for his countrymen. Jerusalem is going to be rebuilt and the temple likewise, the centre of town and country. But there is no trace of any relationship to the priestly caste. And nowhere is the hierarchy, the post-exilic substitute for the lost kingship, alluded to in Second-Isaiah's preaching.

Second-Isaiah is a literary man. The style and composition of his addresses show him to be a man of letters. The text we have may have been enlarged by additions and liturgical insertions, but the abundance of his figurative language and his ability in applying hymns and historical material, without losing sight of his purpose, show his literary faculty.

Any portrayal remains, however, for the greater part vague. Second-Isaiah is in some respects a complex character. Several lines of pre-exilic Israel meet each other in his personality. He is, on the other hand, a new figure in the spiritual life of his people. What is new is, I think, to a great extent determined by the fate of his people in a century full of changes in the world's face.

The forum of Judean experience in this sixth century is world-wide. This wideness is inversely proportionate to the

weakness of a scattered and oppressed people. The interpretation of the revolution did not result in world-wide conceptions but in the narrow form of a renewal of the previous state.
Yhwh is the saviour of his people. Second-Isaiah's message
is thus the starting-point for the religious-nationalistic
conceptions which dominate Judaism.

This narrow application, caused by the situation of the
people and in the next centuries nourished by the attitude
towards the Jewish people of the surrounding nations,
effected more than this religious nationalism. Second-Isaiah's
soteriological thoughts culminate in the idea of vicarious
suffering. It is this idea that originates from the same interpretation of the happenings of his days. It is the inward
spiritual digestion of the confused and bewildering circumstances.

Judaism numbers many members whose religious strength
is nourished by this conception. Christianity has been strongly
related to it since its very beginning. The Gospels pre-
clude every doubt of Jesus' familiarity with Second-Isaiah's
message and the first generations of his disciples interpreted
Jesus' life and death in terms directly borrowed from Second-
Isaiah's message.

"L'homme en tant qu'être historique, concret, authentique
. . . est *en situation*" (ELIADE). The circumstances are a deter-
mining factor of Second-Isaiah's message. They, too, in
Judaism and in Christianity, determine the appropriation of
Second-Isaiah's conceptions. It is the analogy of situation
that decides whether such an appropriation is justifiable
or not.

The historical approach results in distinguishing the
characteristic features of the situation which is studied.
Applications of words and ideas in other times may be justifiable but can never determine the significance of the applied

material. This is all the more cogent in that the Jewish as well as the Christian application of the Bible is to a great extent fixed by a modernizing method of exegesis, rooted in the Jewish conception of the holiness of the Scriptures, a conception never wholly overcome in Christianity. Second-Isaiah's message is only understandable in its own context.

The history of the religious life of mankind shows several epochs in which this part of the Bible has awakened new hope and strength for suffering in life of men in different but analogic situations. For those who know God's punishment and deliverance in their own life, Second-Isaiah is an example of man's ability to interpret his fate as God's purpose. For them Second-Isaiah's message is a unique specimen of Divine Presence, Immanuel.

GECITEERDE AUTEURS

REGISTER VAN BIJBELPLAATSEN